Volume Two of the Electronic Underground Series

THE TELEVISION GRAY MARKET

Henry L. Eisenson

INDEX Publishing Group
San Diego, California

The TELEVISION GRAY MARKET

Published by
INDEX PUBLISHING GROUP
3368 Governor Drive, Suite 273F
San Diego, California 92122

Copyright © 1993 by
INDEX PUBLISHING GROUP
ISBN 1-56866-037-5
Library of Congress Catalog Card Number: 92-75120

Cataloging in Publication

Eisenson, Henry L., 1938-
    The television gray market / Henry L. Eisenson.
    p. cm -- (The electronic underground series ; v. 2)
    Preassigned LCCN: 92-075120
    ISBN 1-56866-037-5

    1. Gray market--United States. 2. Direct broadcast satellite television-
- United States. 3. Cable television--United States. 4. Video recordings--
United States. I Title. II. Series.

TK9960.E57 1993   384.55

                                                            QB193-7

Printed by
SOS Printing, San Diego California
United States of America

3 4 5 6 7 8 9

First printing: November 1992
Second printing: April 1993
Third printing   October 1993

INTRODUCTION

The Electronic Underground^SM Series explores the gray market of electronic equipment that is openly advertised and sold for potentially – perhaps likely – illegal uses. There are many examples... A covert listening device may be entertaining, but such equipment is usually bought for illegal (or at least unethical) eavesdropping. Scanners let hobbyists listen to the world of law enforcement, but many scanners were *designed* to illegally monitor cellular telephones by clipping one wire. The same firms sell radar speed guns to the *police* and radar detectors to *speeders*.

The underground has many parts, of which television is only one. Volume Two of the Series presents the Television Gray Market, including satellite, cable, and videotape media, services, agencies, and products. The Glossary will expand your vocabulary, and the Appendix lists sources of equipment and information. The Television Gray Market is an industry with its own rules. For instance, many members advertise in popular national magazines, yet cannot sell their goods <u>unless</u> the shipment crosses a state line. The cable industry pursues programming thieves, yet unrestricted sale of surplus descramblers, and leakage of new ones, plus open access to scrambling information, support the gray market and make such crimes possible. This is a strange business...

Appearance or mention within this book does not necessarily mean that any company, product, service, author, book, periodical, or editor is violating any law whatever.

CONTENTS

CONTENTS *continued*

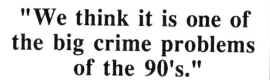

"We think it is one of the big crime problems of the 90's."

Mark Bullock, supervisory special agent, FBI White Collar Crime, responsible for 103 signal theft convictions in 1991.

as reported in *Secure Signals*

8

INDEX PUBLISHING GROUP
San Diego, CA

The Videocipher II uses the Digital Encryption Standard, developed by the National Security Agency to protect our country's most precious secrets. Not even the world's fastest computers can penetrate this technology.

...from a 1985 statement to a TVRO equipment retailer.

SATELLITE TV

Satellite TV basics

"Satellite TV" is often called TVRO, for TeleVision Receive Only. A TVRO system consists of an antenna and receiver on the earth's surface, capable of receiving signals transmitted by satellites more than 22,000 miles overhead and converting those signals to a form that can be used by a conventional television set. This is a complex and expensive process.

In urban markets, population density justifies the cost of installing the "head end" and the cable distribution system. In many parts of the world, including most of rural America, there's no direct broadcast television ("off-air") because of the distance between transmitters and receivers. Millions of potential viewers in rural America represent an important market, despite the fact that many of them work long hours and sleep most of the rest. Marketers and advertisers sought ways to bring to these poor, deprived people the justice of Dragnet re-runs, the security of Sure deodorant, and the bliss of Salem cigarettes... but our planet got in the way.

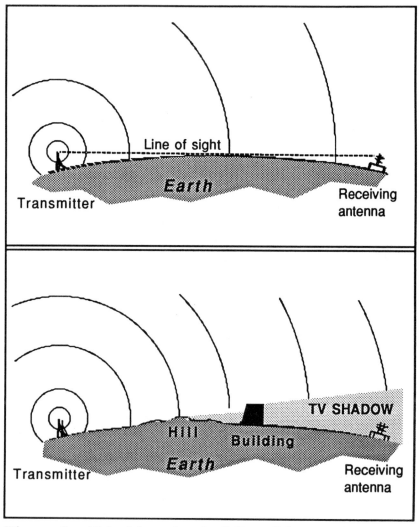

Figure 1: Television signals follow "line of sight," and can be obstructed by buildings, hills, or horizon.

The frequencies at which television stations must broadcast dictate that the signals travel only in perfectly straight lines, which means that for reception to occur, the transmitter and receiver must be connectable by a line that does not intersect any obstacle such as buildings, hills, or the earth itself.

A so-called "network television program," broadcast in many cities at once, was once recorded on film and physically flown to the network stations that would carry it. There was no such thing as "real-time" national news in the '50s, since there was no way to make a simultaneous national broadcast as events occurred. Microwave changed that, and by the '60s many television markets were linked by a complex network of towers and large dish antennas.

Each tower received a microwave signal from a tower just at the line-of-sight limit, amplified it, and retransmitted it to the next tower. This video distribution network was expensive and complex, and was subject to weather problems. It worked, however, and allowed simultaneous national broadcasts and distribution of programming without the delay and risk of physical transport by aircraft. Each network became exactly that, with stations linked together.

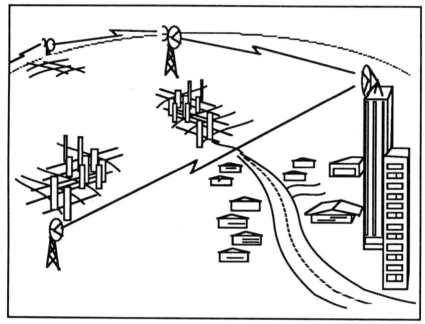

Figure 2: Microwave links cross the countryside.

How satellite TV works

Sputnik's descendants could remain in orbit indefinitely, and it wasn't long before the commercial possibilities of satellite television became very evident. Engineers and accelerating technology quickly made it practical to equip a satellite with solar-powered transponders (a transponder receives a signal on one frequency and re-transmits it on another), and to place it at that critical altitude of about 22,500 miles where it will remain precisely stationary above one point on earth.

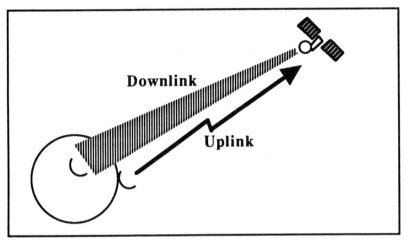

Figure 3: **With the satellite 22,500 miles out, the signal takes a quarter second to travel out and back.**

For each transponder, a ground station first collects and integrates the signal, which might include one television program, several audio programs, plus management or control data for the satellite. That signal is beamed up, not with Scotty's help but by a powerful amplifier and a large dish to focus its energy.

At the geostationary satellite, a special antenna detects that signal and circuitry distributes it appropriately. The video and audio programs are beamed back to earth using a specialized antenna and an amplifier with as little as seven or eight watts output. That signal is "shaped" by the antenna to fit the desired target area, where it is detectable by a dish of 6' to 12' in diameter.

The new technology met an important need of the networks, which quickly developed satellite distribution systems. The network's primary studio would produce a news program which would be amplified and fed to a dish aimed at the satellite overhead. The satellite would receive the program and retransmit it to dishes at all network affiliates, which amplified and rebroadcast to viewers in the market. Cable channels, such as HBO and Showtime, stopped mailing videotapes to their affiliated cable distributors, and instead installed their own network of dishes. Very quickly, the video industry was communicating by satellite link, and a cable company's product consisted of signals from an array of dishes, plus "off-air" programs from local stations.

Though the video-satellite business was originally stimulated by industry requirements, and a TVRO earth station might be far more costly than consumers would be willing to pay, an opportunity was perceived.

Historically, the cost of high-tech performance has dropped over time. It was obvious that to convert state-of-the-art TVRO technology into an expensive consumer product would accelerate that process.

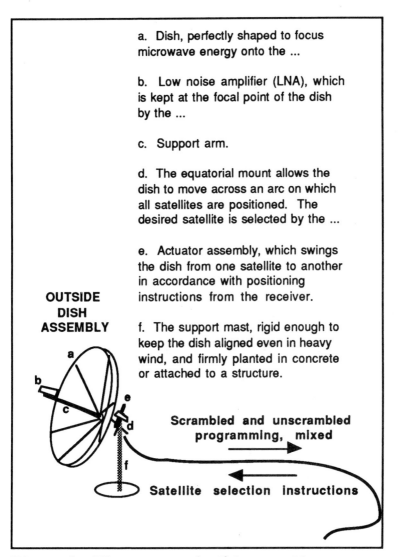

a. Dish, perfectly shaped to focus microwave energy onto the ...

b. Low noise amplifier (LNA), which is kept at the focal point of the dish by the ...

c. Support arm.

d. The equatorial mount allows the dish to move across an arc on which all satellites are positioned. The desired satellite is selected by the ...

e. Actuator assembly, which swings the dish from one satellite to another in accordance with positioning instructions from the receiver.

f. The support mast, rigid enough to keep the dish aligned even in heavy wind, and firmly planted in concrete or attached to a structure.

OUTSIDE DISH ASSEMBLY

Scrambled and unscrambled programming, mixed

Satellite selection instructions

Figure 4: **The consumer's dish assembly.**

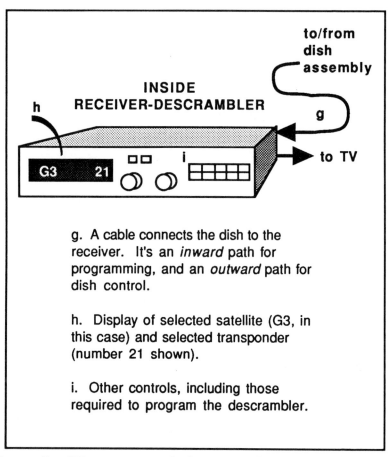

g. A cable connects the dish to the receiver. It's an *inward* path for programming, and an *outward* path for dish control.

h. Display of selected satellite (G3, in this case) and selected transponder (number 21 shown).

i. Other controls, including those required to program the descrambler.

Figure 5: The consumer's indoor unit – the receiver, which includes the electronics required to shift the dish from one satellite to another.

The emergence of consumer TVRO

It wasn't long before entrepreneurs mortgaged their homes, quit their jobs, and began selling Television Receive-Only hardware to the consumer. Expensive, such systems could tune to network broadcasts, broken "feeds" transmitted by distant news teams, and (of course) all of cable television's programming.

Every rural customer who paid the $25-30,000 entry fee suddenly became the most popular farmer in the district. TV by satellite was especially entertaining as the cameras remained fixed upon newscasters who picked their noses and primped while awaiting a cue. Broadcasting was unscrambled and free of local commercials, and to those who once saw TV only rarely, it was fascinating. Statistics might show that the country's agricultural output took a nosedive, but probably omit the cause.

By 1981 prices had dropped by an order of magnitude, and a competent system with a ten-foot dish could be installed for under $5,000. The dishes could be electrically shifted to aim at any of a dozen satellites stretched across the southern sky, each with twenty-four transponders or more, broadcasting hundreds of channels of television. The market for TVRO equipment skyrocketed, dealers were delighted, and on a drive through the countryside one could see more satellite dishes than tractors. Mexico launched its own satellite and began all-Spanish programming, and the "satellite dish" became a south-of-the-border status symbol.

Farm channels appeared on satellite television. Crop reports, rural-focus news, country entertainment, commodity market results, and even telephone auctions of farm equipment, land, horses and cattle, all emerged to support the rural TVRO customer.

Most satellites have 24 transponders, of which each can handle one television channel plus multiple audio channels as well. It was practical to use TVRO to listen to radio news, music, and other audio programming that was available only with a dish. Of the many satellites, few rented time on all 24 transponders, but even at 50 percent usage there were over 150 channels available.

Equipment matured rapidly to couple automatic fine tuning with remote channel and satellite selection; the dedicated channel-hopping consumer could spend hours flipping through channels without revisiting any. Nationwide TVRO schedules were published, equipment manufacturers went public, and the market boomed.

Consumer TVRO began successfully serving its intended market: the rural viewers.

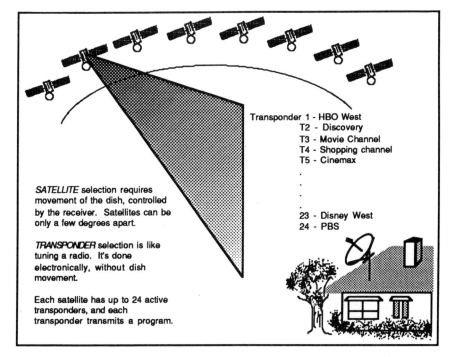

Transponder 1 - HBO West
T2 - Discovery
T3 - Movie Channel
T4 - Shopping channel
T5 - Cinemax
.
.
.
23 - Disney West
24 - PBS

SATELLITE selection requires movement of the dish, controlled by the receiver. Satellites can be only a few degrees apart.

TRANSPONDER selection is like tuning a radio. It's done electronically, without dish movement.

Each satellite has up to 24 active transponders, and each transponder transmits a program.

Figure 6: **Each satellite can simultaneously transmit up to 24 television programs, plus radio – and there are *many* satellites across the sky.**

It didn't take long for some urban customers to recognize that they could buy TVRO equipment, and replace the monthly payment to the cable company with a payment to a loan company – the difference was that the loan could eventually be paid off but the monthly cable bill would come forever. Dishes began appearing in cities, even in areas served by cable. Cable operators supported legislation to prohibit dishes in some communities, but courts felt that this reduced access to information – access guaranteed by the constitution. So dishes continued to proliferate, and the hardware makers prospered.

Rural consumers who once had no TV gained sudden access to hundreds of channels. City users kissed their cable companies goodbye. Hardware-makers were delighted with their sales curves. Local installers grew rapidly and profitably. Advertising executives were pleased by their increased market coverage. Fortunes were made. Legally. Almost everyone was happy with TVRO... *Almost* everyone.

Cable operators *and* the programmers (HBO, etc.) were not happy at all. They were angered by what they perceived as missed revenue, and in 1981 HBO was the first to go to the electronics industry for a solution to their problem. The search for a secure signal pipeline between programmers and their cable operators was supported by the fact that our free market formula permits creation of *both* the demand and the supply. In this example, scrambling would generate not only scrambler sales to programmers and cable operators, but a consumer market for descramblers as well. In effect, the consumer would have to purchase a solution to a problem that was created artificially. Some angry

TVRO owners described the situation as similar to that of a pharmaceutical company that created a disease and then offered vaccines. Nevertheless, and ethics aside, the demand and the supply were created together.

Satellite scrambling and descramblers

Linkabit was a successful San Diego entrepreneurial adventure founded in the 1970s. Initially a specialist in digital signal processing for military communication programs, the company evolved into the electronics industry's premiere innovator in many important technologies, including the digital encryption and decryption of signals. Linkabit's marketers recognized that programmers would welcome a reliable method by which TVRO owners could be charged for the programming they had once received free. The Videocipher technology was conceived to first scramble the satellite's broadcast, and then descramble that signal for paying subscribers.

Each Videocipher descrambler had a secret identity coded within its circuitry. If the satellite's signal contained the right unlocking code for that particular identity, the Videocipher would descramble the signal. By calling an 800-number and providing credit card data plus a unique number displayed by his Videocipher, a viewer could pay for subscriptions to HBO, Showtime, and many other services, and his descrambler would then be "turned on" by the satellite signal itself.

Linkabit proudly announced that the Videocipher was impregnable, as its operation was based upon the Digital Encryption Standard (DES), a coding method developed by the National Security Agency and used as the basis of many critical encryption technologies. DES was so important to our national security that it was actually illegal to export a Videocipher! Few understand how a technology, "critical to national security and barred from export," could be built into an inexpensive consumer product that could be purchased at thousands of outlets nationwide. Nevertheless, the Videocipher was a well-designed, reliable, and relatively economical product, and it did the job – for weeks and weeks.

The Videocipher concept included burying a stream of authorization codes within that portion of the video signal called the "horizontal blanking interval." The information stream was so fast that the individual code for every subscriber across the nation, and the programming for which each paid, could be transmitted in minutes. That process was repeated regularly, and every Videocipher received its specific authorizations early each month, for that month, when it was turned on and tuned to a scrambled channel.

The Videocipher had competition, of course (this is a market-driven society). Products from Sony, Oak, and others were developed. For some who had invested heavily in a TVRO system, and had been watching hundreds of channels free, it made no sense at all that several different and expensive descramblers were required to maintain access to those channels. Quickly, however, the industry gravitated toward the Videocipher, and with a few exceptions, competing hardware became expensive paperweights. This aggravated consumer anger, but there was little recourse. The Videocipher became the industry standard for consumer TVRO, and by 1986 nearly everything "interesting" was scrambled by that system.

Consumer reaction to scrambling

Sales of consumer TVRO hardware plummeted as HBO and other programmers installed scramblers (from Linkabit, of course) and the cable operators installed the corresponding descramblers (also from Linkabit); one by one most useful satellite channels were scrambled. Somehow, even the Public Broadcasting System (PBS) was scrambled! It wasn't necessary to purchase a subscription to PBS because the program was scrambled in such a way that *any* Videocipher would automatically descramble it, without authorization. Nevertheless,

Sesame Street couldn't be watched unless the system was equipped with a Videocipher. The argument was that the Videocipher provided better sound quality than non-scrambled signals, but to many viewers this seemed unfair. There were many other frustrations.

Consumers were further angered to discover that the subscription cost of satellite-delivered television was actually higher than the same programming delivered by cable. This didn't seem fair, since in TVRO it was the consumer who had to make the capital investment in a dish and electronics rather than the cable company running cables through the market, and the consumer had to purchase the descrambler (while cable customers were supplied the same sort of equipment at no charge). Consumers were unhappy to learn that local cable companies would receive a portion of the TVRO customer's subscription payment, whether or not there was access to cable at the customer's location! Dish sales went into free-fall.

Many TVRO sellers and installers went out of business, and what once looked like a profitable industry became a graveyard for entrepreneurs. But help was coming...

The designers made a serious error when they claimed the Videocipher was "absolutely uncrackable," because that statement was a direct challenge. Engineering managers know that one way to solve an "unsolvable" puzzle is to give it to a team of smart young engineers, and simply fail to tell them there is no solution. That may have been one factor in the penetration of Videocipher security, but some believe even today that the Videocipher could never have been cracked without technical help from someone involved its design. There are many myths and fables in the Videocipher saga, including this one: *because TVRO demand fell off so dramatically as scrambling increased, many dealers went out of business. Revenue from descrambler sales dropped to a point where the program's financial plan dictated "leaking" information to those trying to crack the DES puzzle.* There are even suggestions that original Videociphers were designed to permit "back door" access to reprogramming. Such information was probably never leaked deliberately, but nevertheless the Videocipher *was* compromised and that stimulated new growth in hardware sales, and a gray market as well.

Programmers were furious. To tap the consumer market, they had paid heavily for scrambling equipment at their end, yet the system was absolutely not secure.

The surviving TVRO dealers saw an almost immediate surge in sales, and Videociphers were routinely sold with all subscription services turned on. Many honest citizens became programming thieves overnight, and there were arguments to help them rationalize their decisions. Philosophical "justification" (aggressively supported by gray marketeers) included these points:

A citizen should be entitled to use anything that falls upon his property, including satellite signals.

Subscription charges were an unregulated rip-off, and were clearly unfair for more reasons than one. Pricing neglected the fact that the consumer had to buy his own equipment, making the capital investment ordinarily made by the cable operator.

Subscription "packages" were pushed heavily, forcing consumers to buy services they neither wanted nor needed.

Pricing was based on the (correct) assumption that many descrambler owners were cheating, which infuriated those who weren't and stimulated them to seek equity.

The consumer buys the descrambler and should have the right to do as he wishes with his own property.

Why should anyone have to buy a Videocipher to watch the Public Broadcasting System?

It is the programmers' responsibility to scramble in such a way that the consumer cannot receive without paying. Any video transmission is "scrambled" in a sense because it is viewable only with special equipment (a TV set). What's the difference when that required "equipment" is a modified descrambler?

Lawmakers ignored the TVRO consumer, as evidenced by the unfair legislation driven home by the cable lobbies. Therefore, it's not really a crime if the act rectifies a wrong.

It was easy to construct such arguments, but the bald fact is that theft of programming was and is a crime, and users of modified Videociphers were technically criminals. The obvious solutions were to place the burden on the engineers ("the technology *must* be made undefeatable") or to change legislation to decriminalize signal theft, and there were attempts to do both, but such scattered efforts stood no chance against the cable lobbies, and the law was carefully shaped to benefit only the business side of the equation.

Most collective decisions made in the TVRO market go through the Satellite Broadcasting Communications Association (SBCA), near Washington, D.C., which can be reached at 703-549-6990 (for literature, etc.). This group supports pro-industry lobbying in the nation's capitol, works to enhance communications between enforcement agencies, and supports broadcasters that use satellite broadcasting as a medium. The SBCA's lobbying is highly effective, and most legislation and decisions to date have been decidedly pro-industry.

An angry consumer group was organized and led by the late Shaun Kenny, a rebel who took on the SBCA, the programmers, and the scrambling industry. At first wildly irreverent and very angry, with an introduction that included a shot of a Videocipher in a urinal, Mr. Kenny's programming mellowed with time and lawsuits. When he was sued by the scramblers, many equally indignant TVRO viewers contributed to his defense fund. He then broadcast a low-key video magazine called *Boresight News*, and an equipment swap meet he called *Greensheet*. These programs moved from one transponder to another, but as late as mid-1992 were seen on Galaxy 6. For many years Mr. Kenny was entertaining and informative, and upon observing his programs one wished that his obviously audacious off-camera comments were audible. Whether he was right or wrong, his saga was a cauldron of constitutional issues.

However the reality was camouflaged or rationalized, consumer greed was always an important part of the picture, because a few hundred dollar investment in a modified descrambler produced unlimited access to an incredible array of programming, such as:

Two broadcasts (east coast and west coast) for each of HBO, Showtime, The Movie Channel, Cinemax, Disney, plus one channel of Playboy

All major sports events, whether or not blacked out on local television.

All "package" cable channels, including CNN, Headline News, Discovery Channel, The Learning Channel, Superstations, and more.

Programming in many languages.

Live horse races (that's how the video makes it to the betting arenas in Vegas).

Hard and soft core pornography.

Network feeds to local affiliates.

Pay-Per-View first-release films.

Network news feeds, as it happens (unedited, and including interesting candid shots of the reporters!).

Hundreds of channels of audio programming.

...and much, much more.

The cost of legitimate subscriptions for all subscribable programming was as much as $1,000 per year – and that did not include Pay-Per-View movies and special sports events. Greed was *indeed* a factor and still is, and over a half million Videocipher units have been modified by those who created an industry to support that greed, amplified by frustration, and justified by self-serving philosophy and rationalization.

At the other end of the pipeline is the programming, which is quite remarkable. As of mid-1992 there are about 25 C-band and 20 Ku-band transponder arrays in orbit (a few satellites have some of both). About 500 transponders are active at one time or another, with regular programming appearing on about 200, of which half are scrambled. The rest of the transponders carry occasional feeds. That is an impressive menu of programming, and it creates enormous market "suction" at the consumer end of the gray market pipeline.

Satellite equipment "modification"

By most opinions, more than half of all Videociphers sold before 1991 have been modified, and most still work. Over the years, Videocipher has gone through many evolutionary iterations, but all work on the same basic principles. The actual descrambler portion of the

Videocipher was avoided by the gray market, which targeted the circuitry and data stream that controlled it.

Schematics, books, pamphlets, and articles have long been on the gray market, and there are no longer any secrets of the inner workings of the Videocipher. Even relatively novice technicians are conversant in the technologies of the supersecret DES. Videocipher designers had met an interesting technical challenge: security had to remain intact regardless of how much was known about the system.

The Videocipher combines elements of information to turn on its internal descrambler for a particular channel. Its unique identity code, buried within an internal chip, is combined digitally with authorization instructions embedded in the horizontal blanking interval of the video signal beamed to earth from the satellite. That is, the satellites were continuously sending not only programming, but also authorization information to hundreds of thousands of Videociphers. The ingredients for authorization were (1) correct identity, (2) a partial descrambling instruction, and (3) the rest of the instructions plus specific authorization, channel by channel. This is a complex process, and defeating it took great technical skill. Actually, the video was as simple to descramble as a cable signal – the majority of the challenge involved descrambling the audio.

The first generation of Videocipher (the "010" version) was naively and confidently introduced to the market, and it took very little time for the first modifications to appear. The manufacturer responded to that by adding epoxy over the chips that had to be modified, and the gray market countered by openly selling a solvent for the epoxy (claiming the epoxy creates heat problems and should be removed). The next generation of equipment – the 018 model – was called "uncrackable, based on years of experience with the piracy industry." Actually, it only took weeks before modification products were developed and services resumed advertising. Many of the original 010 units had been purchased and stockpiled by the pirate industry, so business remained good even when the manufacturer went to the "018" and then the "032" model. Before the inventory of each level was depleted, the following unit was compromised.

Original Videociphers were housed in a separate box about the size of a satellite receiver. That box contained a power supply, control circuitry, and the Videocipher module. Today, that module is inserted into Integrated Receiver-Descrambler (IRD) products, which combine the receiver and descrambler functions in one unit. In all cases, it is that module that is attacked; the remainder of the receiver provides no descrambling functions. Whether by Houston Tracker, Toshiba, or any other IRD manufacturer, the "*D*" in the name is the

Videocipher Descrambler. The "Videocipher" is that internal module used in all IRDs...

Videociphers have a finite lifetime. Memory (including identity) is powered by an internal lithium battery that most believe will last less than ten years. When that battery dies and AC power is disconnected, even for a moment, the Videocipher loses its identity and becomes "brain-dead." This can happen when a circuit breaker trips, when the unit is transported, when power drops, etc. Once it happens, the unit can be resuscitated only by a modifier able to install a valid identification code. As older units die out they are replaced by newer designs more difficult and costly to modify. The gray market has gotten around the battery issue. Some firms offer a replacement nickel-cadmium battery that is kept charged by the circuit, with the wiring necessary to keep the battery charged, and exquisitely detailed instructions to prevent inadvertent de-powering of the memory circuitry while the battery is being installed.

The fundamental challenge faced by gray market engineers was to convince the descrambler that it should do its job.

The first method used was "cloning," where services would be bought for one Videocipher identity, but a multitude of units would be modified to correspond to that identity code. The "Three Musketeers" method required that the subscriber purchase at least one subscription, but the modified Videocipher would use that enabling code to authorize all services – hence *"one for all and all for one."* Another technique simply "turned on" everything by independently generating its own unique authorization codes. In the meantime, programmers boiled. Many magazines carried open, unambiguous ads for chips, modules, and modification services. A satellite program analyzed VCII circuitry and offered repair and modification tips, and at least one company sold videotapes with step-by-step procedures for modifying the descrambler.

The product evolved, and Videocipher changed hands. As Linkabit was purchased by M/A-Com, the product line was sold to General Instruments (GI), also a San Diego company. GI now sells yet another version of the design, and in the eyes of some programmers has begun taking seriously the problem of piracy. The news media show evidence that there has been an effort to identify suppliers of goods and services and take them to court, often with help of the federal Attorney General plus local law enforcement agencies, but also (reportedly) with private investigators. Of course, it doesn't take Sherlock Holmes to find these suppliers when they advertise every month in national magazines. Some have been advertising their Videocipher-cracking wares for many years, with unambiguous claims, addresses, credit card financing, 800-numbers, and faxes. They have never been hard to find or identify.

The gray market's product line evolved to include much more than just chips for descramblers. Entrepreneurs offered solvents for epoxy, manuals and videotapes, magazines, tools, battery kits, cables to permit surgery on the module when it was removed from the Videocipher chassis, training programs, consulting services, methods for encrypting customer files, and many more products and services – which were advertised in newsletters and even on programs broadcast on satellite. Since the introduction of the first Videocipher, this has grown into big business, and shutting it down will be difficult.

General Instruments is trying, and the first fundamental change in TVRO descramblers is the Videocipher II+, which appears in all new IRDs by all manufacturers shipped as of mid-1992. Today, the modification dealers simply replace that module with an older one that has been modified. This can not last forever, as measures and countermeasures continue to see-saw. As the number of TVRO viewers grows, so does the financial pressure to improve security.

Some observers have made unsubstantiated claims that there were always ways to make an uncrackable Videocipher, but then hardware sales would fall. Both GI and Linkabit may now believe that the TVRO market has reached critical mass, and it's time for designs that will not be defeated. The fall-1992 news is that as Linkabit's not-to-compete covenant expires, Linkabit (now owned by Titan) and Houston Tracker will support a joint venture to produce a Videocipher that reportedly will sell for less than the GI unit.

Of course, these battles have little to do with the B-MAC scrambling system, by Scientific Atlanta, which protects sporting events and movies transmitted to hotel and institutional customers in the U. S., and was adopted by major satellite programmers in Australia. B-MAC is a sophisticated descrambler that can cost more than $2,000, including modifications. B-MAC signals were never intended for the U. S. consumer, so those stealing such signals cannot use the rationalization and indignation that often support Videocipher-based piracy.

There are other scrambling-descrambling technologies in use today. MacroVision is a new technique used for sports feeds. The Leitch system supports primarily industrial video, but was cloned anyway. Oak-Orion is popular in Canada and is occasionally used for sporting events in the United States, and reports predict a new upgrade that requires renewable security (credit card) authorization. There is little U. S. consumer use of this second-tier descrambler hardware, and therefore little financial pressure to develop gray market products.

Direct Broadcast Satellite (DBS)

DBS systems are scheduled to go into service in 1994, and will operate at a much higher frequency than the existing satellite systems. As frequency increases, the required size of the antenna goes down for a given level of performance. An antenna technique called "phased array" allows electronic steering of non-mobile flat antennas. The new DBS systems exploit these advantages, and will use very small (perhaps two-foot) flat antennas that can be mounted almost anywhere, even on an apartment window. DBS will depend upon descrambler technology much like that used today, and shortly after its introduction will probably spawn a gray market of its own.

Industry countermeasures and consumer risk

Experts today believe that about 500,000 to 750,000 illegal Videociphers are in use at a premium (above the price of the basic descrambler) of about $250 each, which defines a $150,000,000 hardware gray market. They also believe that programmers are losing about

$250,000,000 per year in lost subscription fees. Those figures create and sustain a market for new technology on both sides of the legal fence. The numbers also support substantial enforcement effort.

Hundreds of thousands of Americans became criminals when they bought and used modified descrambler equipment to steal programming. To access that programming they had to purchase a Videocipher, so it was only the programmers who lost revenues due to program piracy – Videocipher manufacturers thrived on this gray market and placated programmers with one temporary solution after another.

While the manufacturers and distributors of illegal hardware are justifiably law enforcement targets, the individual consumer was rarely investigated even when there was a higher than 50-50 chance that *any* dish was wired to an illegally modified descrambler.

If he buys a cloned unit and the enforcement agencies discover its hidden identity code (by purchasing one from the same dealer network, for instance), instead of an authorization signal the programmers can add to the data stream an instruction for that particular code to "go brain dead." That, of course, effectively "kills" every unit in which a cloning process has inserted that same identity code. Since the signal is from a satellite, the command affects all such units in use, in any location.

The risk to the consumer is primarily financial. There are very few cases on record where even an obviously guilty consumer, perhaps turned in by an angry girlfriend, was convicted of anything or even had his *legal* equipment confiscated, unless he were actively involved in the gray market. The legitimate side of the business believed that the consumer, threatened sufficiently, would become a paying customer who would buy a legal descrambler and begin subscribing. History validates that view for the most part, but when a consumer was caught a decision had to be made regarding the propaganda value of a conviction. When caught, most consumers were converted into revenue, but some made the news as a deterrent. In most such cases, a clever attorney found it easy to reach a compromise by which the scrambling forces achieved their propaganda goals without serious penalty to the consumer. Such legal issues and propaganda efforts were insignificant when compared to the problems involved in the control of information.

The iron curtain is down, but spies still challenge counterspies in the television gray market, with both sides driven by hundreds of millions of dollars of financial pressures in each direction. Some of the stories read like Ludlum's best. In the mid-1980's, one entrepreneur offered a training course in Videocipher modification, conducted in the Bahamas. Investors paid thousands of dollars to travel there, where they were instructed in the latest modification process and given chips to act as models in their gray market businesses. When they got off their plane in Florida, however, the FBI confiscated their materials and charges were filed. Many believe that at least one of the students was a plant, inserted by the SBCA or another member of the legitimate side of the industry.

Across the country, the FBI has assisted private detectives and employees of SBCA members in first identifying and then raiding modification services, hardware sellers, and even – in a very few cases – multi-level marketers who were recovering the cost of their own modified descramblers by selling to friends.

In some cases, a raid put the accused out of business completely even if there was insufficient evidence collected to convict (which means, in the United States, that the accused was "innocent"). All test equipment, computers, software, and customer files, plus inventory, would be confiscated, and it sometimes took so long to determine criminality (or the lack of it) that the suspect simply could not recover.

And many *were* guilty. Across the country, vendors of TVRO systems couldn't compete unless they would take responsibility not only for the warranty on the hardware, but also for the "fix" on the Videocipher. As the industry implemented anti-piracy measures, the dealer would install the next countermeasure, etc.

On the other side of the fence industrial espionage thrived. Legends abound about secret meetings where descrambler and software information was exchanged for cash, with careful protection of identities. Gray marketeers hired professional engineering groups to map a path to the fully-authorized promised land.

The Videocipher II+ was designed with room to grow. The first circuit boards of this class included the VCII+ descrambler only, and Pay-Per-View was added later. The version shipped today includes those functions plus a Renewable Security capability that requires a "smart card" for periodic reactivation. According to most experts, the VCII+ has not been compromised and is replacing older designs. If the VCII data stream is shut down late in 1992, as many predict, only the "plus" version will know where to find its instructions.

The Videocipher II+ looks for its authorization data not in the horizontal blanking interval of the video signal, but in the *vertical* interval. As long as broadcasts contain authorization in both locations, the old and the new Videociphers will work, but if/when the authorization is removed from the horizontal interval, the older style Videociphers will become useless. General Instruments permits owners of legitimate Videocipher units to exchange their modules for the newer design at no cost, hoping this will leave programming pirates out in the cold. Owners of *modified* modules will have to purchase new ones at prices up to $500 – enough business from those transactions will compensate General Instruments for the no-charge exchange of legitimate descramblers.

Measures and countermeasures may continue forever, driven by the economics of programming piracy. Videocipher sales plus the cost of illegal hardware add to numbers that are very persuasive to those willing to enter this illegal market. When the VCII data stream is vacated, the 500,000+ owners of modified older descramblers will instantly become a market worth up to $250,000,000 to the makers of legitimate VCII+ instruments, and even more to the gray market if/when it is successful in defeating the VCII+ technology.

Assuming that the Videocipher II+ is eventually compromised, the "Renewable Security" subsystem will be actuated. The VCII+ RS includes that circuitry, which requires periodic renewal of the descrambler scheme with a credit card mailed to paying subscribers.

The first of such "smart card" systems were employed in Europe, however, where it is derided by some gray marketeers as a "dumb" card, and is reputed to have been quickly compromised.

The gray market brings vast resources to the new challenge, and if the new Videocipher technology *can* be compromised, it *will be*. The gray market combination of technical skill and financial pressure is a powerful force. An author of a VCII modification guide said recently, "whoever first cracks a new VCII scheme makes millions." But no patents will be issued on illegal technologies, and there is no honor among thieves. The developer of any new cracking technique can be certain that his competitors will be among his first customers, and they will instantly begin offering the same product to the same market. The gray marketeers are not only vulnerable to the law, but to each other.

The latest information from the gray market is that the VCII+ *has* been compromised such that entrepreneurs are now offering to transfer authorization codes to a consumer's VCII+ by telephone modem. The war continues...

The TVRO industry's best solutions have never changed: the tasks are to (1) develop a scrambling technology that is difficult and expensive to penetrate, and (2) lower the cost of TVRO programming to reduce frustration and temptation. With the introduction of the Videocipher II+ and the RS capability, it appears that the first of these steps has been attempted. If the new descramblers are not quickly defeated by the gray market, programmers may ultimately reduce subscription prices to reflect that fact. Though a first, such a step will lower the pressures on the gray market to defeat the VCII+, and on the consumer to cheat. Combined with effective enforcement and a reasonable consumer education program, these steps have the potential to terminate the TVRO gray market.

The consumer will continually compare the cost of cheating (including penalties if caught) to the cost of subscribing, and will make his decisions based more on economics than morality.

The primary method, therefore, by which this segment of the gray market will be shut down is pricing by the programmers and cable companies. If their prices reflect success of the new security measures, the consumer's motivation will diminish along with the gray market's incentive to invest in still further counter-counter-countermeasures.

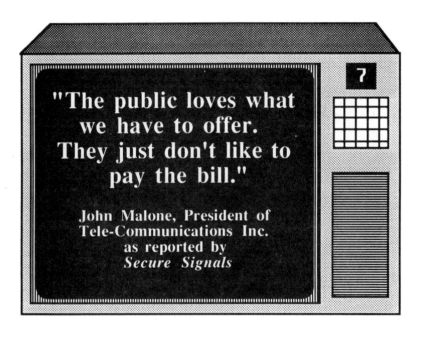

"The public loves what we have to offer. They just don't like to pay the bill."

John Malone, President of Tele-Communications Inc.
as reported by
Secure Signals

"Who's watching
the watchers?
**90% of our
inventory comes directly from
the cable companies! They'll
ship to anyone... even me.**"

*Vendor of descramblers that "can
only be sold across state lines."*

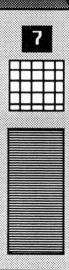

CABLE TV

Cable TV basics

Cable television began in the 1940s when television retailers avoided interference and improved viewing by establishing a well-located master antenna, and then amplifying and distributing the video signal to customers' homes by cable.

From a fairly meager start fifty years ago, cable is becoming the dominant mechanism by which video programming reaches the consumer. In 1950 there were 70 cable TV operations in the United States, serving a total of about 15,000 subscribers. By late 1987 there were nearly 11,000 cable companies serving more than 22.5 million subscribers in nearly 27,000 communities. Those figures have increased greatly in the last five years. The average cable system today has approximately 4,000 subscribers (of whom about 200, statistically, actively steal programming).

As the technology evolved, broadcasts from relatively distant and hard-to-receive stations were included. Eventually, premium services such as HBO entered the

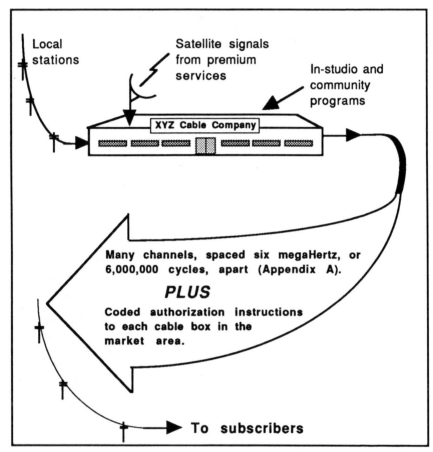

Figure 7: The content of a cable signal.

scene and charged an optional higher fee for movies and special productions. That practice defined a huge business opportunity that has grown into a medium at least as popular and influential as the "free" broadcast networks. Today, the preponderance of cable programming is of the premium variety rather than from conventional broadcast stations or networks.

Each such premium programmer buys or creates program material and transmits it to a satellite (the "uplink") more than 22,000 miles above the earth, to be retransmitted down in a pattern that covers the entire country (See Chapter 1).

The signal for an area is received by the distribution company that owns the right to sell programming to it. That company's building is studded with dish antennas because most of their programming is received from satellites. The distribution company receives those channels, adds local television services received by wire or produced internally, and combines everything into a single composite signal that contains scrambled and unscrambled channels mixed together. That multi-channel transmission is the "product" sold by the cable company and distributed throughout its market, but getting it onto a television screen is no simple matter.

The cable company transmits the signal to each neighborhood by various means – microwave transmission, electronic cable, or glass fiber (fiber optic cable), are examples. Electronic conversion circuitry changes the transmission into true cable signals, preserving scrambling, and sends it to distribution units that amplify the signal and feed it to cables either buried or held aloft by utility poles in the street. From that line, individual feeds go to each house. Every account is electrically isolated from others so that a short-circuit in one home (from a cut or improperly crimped cable, for instance) will not affect reception in others. Multiple residence buildings often have a single feed, which is then amplified and distributed throughout the structure. Erroneously called "CATV" (see Glossary), some buildings pay for service and include it in the rent or association fee.

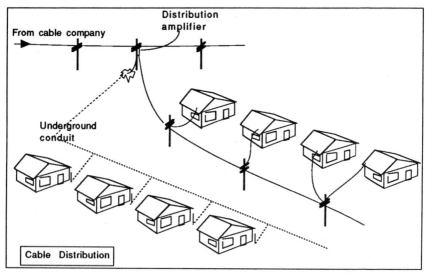

Figure 8: **The cable may be hung on poles or buried.**

The cable that enters each home carries all channels, scrambled or otherwise, mixed together as a complex signal, and also carries authorization information to the thousands or even millions of cable boxes in the network. The "cable box" resting atop the television set is much like a radio – it can "tune" a single program from the many that are available to it – it selects the desired program from that complex combined signal and sends it into the television set – perhaps on channel 3 or 4, perhaps as a separate pair of video and audio signals fed to connectors at the rear of the television set.

The cable box also receives and decodes the cable company's authorization instruction that was mixed in with the video programming. The cable carries all such instructions to all cable boxes in the market, but each unit recognizes and reacts to *only* the authorization that contains its specific address code. Your cable box can therefore be instructed by the cable company to descramble only those channels for which you've paid. The descrambler section of the cable box restores some critical part of the video signal (audio is usually not disturbed) so your television set can stabilize the picture and make it viewable.

In most cable systems, one subscription channel – usually HBO – can be received with no cable box (descrambler), because instead of scrambling the signal the cable company's technician *installs* a simple filter to remove that channel from the cable as it enters your home, or *removes* a filter that prevents a confusing signal to enter with the premium channel. When the filter is changed, that channel is "turned ON" for all the outlets within the home simultaneously, which is why a subscription to HBO (or any premium channel blocked using a filter technique) provides service to all TV sets in the home, which also means that there is no parental control over programming unless extra hardware is added. Other premium services require a separate descrambler – and the purchase of separate subscriptions – for each television set.

Downconverters and descramblers

The cable signal enters the structure and goes to all outlets throughout the home. One outlet might go to a "cable-ready" television set that tunes cable signals, another to a downconverter wired to a non-cable-ready television set, and a third to a converter/descrambler (permits reception of all premium services that are authorized, or "turned on"). As mentioned before, HBO is authorized by the removal or addition of a small filter assembly on the cable, usually where the cable enters the customer's structure.

Several such filter-based systems might be used. One is called a "trap," which is a filter that blocks the appropriate channel's frequency from appearing at its output (see Appendix A and Glossary). A "reverse trap" blocks a special signal that confuses the tuner, thus allowing the premium channel to be tuned. Many companies sell such filters (traps) to the cable consumer for prices ranging from $16 to $20 – or about the cost of one month of HBO – and most of those companies can assist the buyer in selecting the specific frequency and type of filter to be used in his market. The same companies often sell the specialized tools used by the cable company to remove and install filters. There are few uses for such filters and tools except to bypass the cable company's security system. Also, some consumers have discovered that by simply cutting the cable prior to a trap-type filter, and then wiring around the trap with simple connectors, they can recover the premium channel. Of course, such modifications are easily detected by simple visual inspection of the box where the cable enters the home. Whether filtered or not, the signal that enters the customer's structure is then distributed to desired locations within the structure.

Apartments and condominiums are often handled in a "block" manner, and modern buildings are pre-wired when built. The cable company offers a discount when all residents in the building subscribe, and each is connected to basic service automatically when he moves in. Any that desire to receive premium services require subscriptions and descramblers. Of course, the feed to each apartment might also have a filter-controlled premium channel.

Most cable companies assess a separate charge for every outlet (they install and know about). Of course, the consumer who can navigate to a Radio Shack can buy "splitters" and run his own cables to wherever required. A cable-ready television set, or an acquired converter, completes the circuit. In almost all areas, the consumer is contractually obligated to pay for additional outlets regardless of who owns the box or who did the work of adding outlets. It is nearly impossible for the cable company to determine how many outlets are installed in a given household without entering the property to make a visual inspection. The installation of an unauthorized outlet is a simple, almost thoughtless, step that violates the consumer's contract with the cable company, and may become his first step toward criminality.

The next step, of course, is to acquire a descrambler for the unauthorized outlet. Of course, it cannot come from the cable company.

Cable boxes are made by many manufacturers, in many forms and styles. Zenith, Jerrold, Scientific Atlanta,

Oak, Pioneer, and others appear throughout North America, but all work on about the same principles. Each cable company was "sold" on equipment from one manufacturer or another, and the selected brand is used in that firm's market.

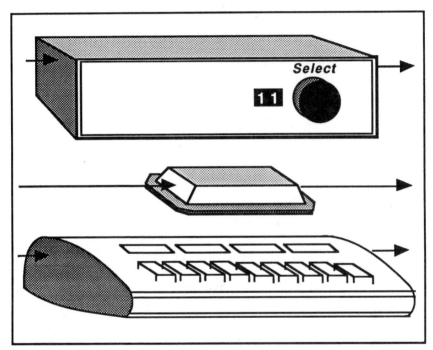

Figure 9: Simple cable converters. The *INPUT* is a cable signal, and the *OUTPUT* is a signal tunable by a television set (see Appendix A). With a cable-ready VCR or TV, such a converter is unnecessary.

Simple downconverters are issued by the cable company when the subscriber pays only for basic services (though usually at least one premium channel can be controlled by a filter in the cable line) and does not want remote control. Most subscribers require a combination downconverter/descrambler, which accomplishes both tasks. Such devices are typically rented, with an additional charge for remote control. There are many different brands of equipment, with only limited compatibility. That is, a given downconverter will not work in all systems, and no descrambler will decode all signals.

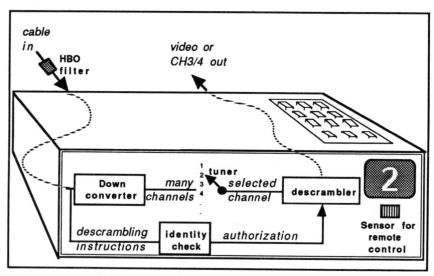

Figure 10: **Typical downconverter-descrambler combination.**

It is easy to determine what downconverter/descrambler is used in a given area by examining a neighbor's unit and recording the manufacturer and model number. With few exceptions, only the correct box will work with each scrambling technique. Some dealers know which unit is used in each zip code across the country.

Current downconverter/descrambler designs include many functions, and are fairly complex. The channel separation circuitry is a tuning mechanism that has little to do with descrambling, as can be seen by switching across all channels, including the premium services to which no subscription exists. It's easy to tune to those channels, and the audio is usually excellent, but the video is smeared and distorted. All video passes through the descrambler circuitry, which looks for authorization before it adds the missing information that makes the video viewable.

Authorization can be transmitted for any service and for any period, from a month or more to a few hours (for Pay-Per-View, for instance). For customers without an addressable descrambler, some systems use self-destructing filters to authorize one Pay-Per-View program. They're ordered by phone, invoiced with the cable bill or paid for by credit card, delivered by mail, and installed by the consumer just before the beginning of a special program, such as a wrestling ballet. Some hours later the filter "dies" and is discarded. For reference, the cable company pays about $10 for filters activated by an internal lithium battery (one is patented by Intercept Communications Products, Inc.).

Conventional premium channel scrambling is different. In most situations and markets, cable companies leave the audio undisturbed, as many subscribers have discovered when their children tune to a scrambled adult program. The scramblers destabilize the video and make it unviewable, and fortunately it is not necessary to understand that technology to use a descrambler and view cable television. It is also not necessary to understand that technology to *steal* video services. Many services and vendors will help the consumer who decides to illegally dodge payment for programming.

Cable equipment modification

"Self-destructing" Pay-Per-View filters are easily copied. An electronic technician can determine the characteristics of such a filter (while it's alive) with a common laboratory instrument called a network analyzer, and the filter can then be duplicated by referring to a filter design manual and plugging the parameters into cookbook procedures. The gray market, however, provides a much easier way to cheat. Consumers can defeat such scrambling by simply calling a distributor via his 800-number. Some know enough to ask for the consumer's credit card number and zip code, and by referring to a computer will identify and ship the correct filter model number for that area. It's legal to build such filters, and to sell them, and to buy them, and to own them. The legal membrane is penetrated when such a legally-acquired device is used to steal services – and there are few other uses for such a filter.

Ongoing theft of services requires a modified cable descrambler. Many gray market companies offer cable boxes that are already internally modified to descramble all channels, paid for or not. Others sell "test chips," which are then inserted within the box by the consumer to produce permanent authorization. Such illegal descramblers can work in several ways.

The earliest descramblers could be defeated by merely cutting or adding a wire, but both measures and countermeasures quickly moved past that, and today's descramblers contain considerable computing power, are digitally addressable, and are very difficult to compromise. The initial cracking technique for such addressable units was the "clone." Subscriptions are purchased to permit one descrambler to legally receive all services, and that descrambler's coded address is placed within the legitimate authorization data stream distributed on the cable. The clone-maker simply opens the descrambler and uses readily available electronic test equipment to read the code that is embedded in memory chips. That identity code is then inscribed on blank chips of the correct type, and those chips are either sold or installed in non-authorized descramblers.

With cloning, for one subscription payment there could be hundreds or thousands of descramblers receiving premium channels. This technique is dangerous to the gray marketeer since it implies commerce within a specific market, because the unique coded identity is authorized by the *local* data stream from the *local* cable company. That means that cloning can work only within a community, and the legal barrier created by a state line isn't available to the pirate, who is therefore exposed to prosecution. And they *are* prosecuted.

More sophisticated techniques are currently in favor. Test equipment determines exactly what signal is sent by an authorized instruction interpreter to the descrambler circuitry, and then a chip is developed to duplicate that signal perfectly. When installed, the descrambler thinks it's been authorized, and operates accordingly. Such technology is sold using the euphemism "test chip," ostensibly to companies that service descramblers but in actuality the "test chip" suppliers rarely ask for credentials. Such a chip can be easily inserted in a descrambler to fool it into descrambling all services. It's a five minute task.

There are few legitimate uses for such test devices. Repairs are properly made by technicians of the cable company or manufacturer, who test the unit by first applying a cable signal with an authorization command buried within it, and then observing the result.

It's easy to understand that cable theft is a thriving business, and like other successful businesses there is a lot of competition. Blatant advertising even appears in national periodicals:

Our Jerrold, Zenith, Oak, and Panasonic cable descramblers are already modified and are absolutely bulletproof! It is your responsibility to notify your cable company of the premium channels you watch, and to buy subscriptions accordingly. (phone #).

SOLD FOR TEST PURPOSES ONLY! Our latest generation test chips will turn on your Zenith SSAVI descrambler to permit checking of all-channel reception. Easy to install without soldering. Quantity 1 @ $35, 100 @ $21, all COD. Guaranteed! (name of company and phone #).

Bulletproof your cable box! Our $29.95 protection circuit prevents countermeasures from interfering with your television reception. Sent COD or use VISA/Mastercard. Guaranteed! (phone #).

These ads appear in many national periodicals, including *Popular Communications*, *Video Review*, *Radio Electronics*, and *Nuts & Volts*.

They should not be confused with semi-legitimate advertisements for *unmodified* descramblers, which are properly acquired only from cable companies, but in fact are sold freely by retailers everywhere - but *not* to customers within their state because of state law forbidding such sales. Remember, it is not possible to buy a descrambler without violating the typical cable contract or, in many states, breaking a state law.

> *Why rent your cable box? Buy it, and never pay rent again! We stock all brands, including Zenith, Oak, Panasonic, Scientific Atlanta, Jerrold, and others, most with remote. These units will receive all channels including Pay-Per-View, when authorized, and it is your responsibility to notify the cable company. All our products are warranted by the manufacturer. Visa/Mastercard/AmEx or COD. (Company name, "800" phone #). No sales in ——.*

This advertisement makes no claims regarding all-channel reception *without* authorization. In a sense, it's deceptive because it implies that the units are able to receive all channels – and some readers will miss the "*when authorized*" clause because they'll see what they want to see. Of course, if the consumer wishes to purchase a "legal" downconverter to go with his "illegal" extra outlets, this sort of supplier is a good source. There is little likelihood that purchasers of such out-of-state boxes will advise their cable companies, most of whom specifically exclude such arrangements in their service contracts with their customers.

Those companies that sell unmodified descramblers usually include disclaimers in their advertising, and almost always cannot sell to customers within their own state – because most states have passed legislation that protect cable operators *within* that state. When a Florida customer calls a Florida supplier he is told that they cannot do business; he is often given the phone number of a supplier *outside* Florida. Assuming a reciprocal arrangement, advertising is not wasted.

Some descramblers are difficult to buy. Pioneer, for instance, has told cable companies that their hardware will be shipped only to legitimate customers, though the name frequently appears in gray market advertising. The latest version of Pioneer equipment, by the way, employs seven levels of security and is reportedly very difficult to defeat. Even removing the cover from the Pioneer unit renders it totally dead, and returning it to the cable company for service can generate a stiff fee. The nature of the gray market has produced a solution, however. Reportedly, the Pioneer descrambling protocol also appears in some models by Scientific Atlanta that have relatively lower security. Again, there are measures and countermeasures, all driven by money.

Some cable companies estimate that programming theft occurs in over five percent of the homes in their markets, not including theft of sports programming by bars and clubs. These numbers brightly illuminate the force driving this gray market. Assume that the actual number is 5%, and that there are 40 million cable installations. That equates to 2,000,000 illegal systems, for which consumers paid an average of about $300.

Illegal cable equipment sales have probably grossed more than $600,000,000! If equipment replacement or market growth produces sales equal to only 10% per year, that's a $60,000,000 market. It's no wonder magazines are full of advertising – a 5% advertising budget is worth $3,000,000. These are staggering numbers, and they define a huge industry.

What's the financial motivation to catch or convert these people? Some members of the cable industry estimate that stolen services are worth $250,000,000 annually, but calculation shows that's not even close. Each thief probably pays for basic cable service, and if he had no illegal descrambler he might subscribe to one or two premium services, but certainly would not pay for all of the services that he had pirated. In most markets, the difference probably averages about $20 per month. For 5% of the market, or two million subscribers, that difference is $40,000,000 per month, or $480,000,000 per year.

These astonishing numbers support a war.

Industry countermeasures and consumer risk

The cable services are aware that they are losing a lot of money through theft of programming, and their lobbies have worked hard in support of legislation to criminalize such activities. The economics of the situation may justify a search for those who sell chips or modification services, but it is rarely cost-effective to expend effort to catch the individual consumer unless persuasive evidence arrives free. After all, the actual loss is probably $20 per month per thief. On the other hand, cable companies work to create the image of a vast detective organization peering through windows, or super electronic testers that can pinpoint just who is watching what – these measures may be possible but they are unlikely, except to create news that is intended to deter signal piracy by the consumer.

The National Cable Television Association (at 1724 Massachusetts Avenue N.W., Washington, DC 20036) is a national association of cable programming suppliers. That organization has created a group called Coalition Opposing Signal Theft (COST), to coordinate and report actions against signal thieves. COST publishes a useful monthly newsletter called *Secure Signals*, which includes articles on anti-theft practices and convictions of cable thieves, plus announcements of meetings, etc. This newsletter is not seen by either gray marketeers or their customers, so it is unclear why such lists of convictions are published, unless COST believes such articles will convince its subscribers that *something* is being done.

Secure Signals is made up of four two-sided 8.5" x 11" plain-paper pages. Two recent issues were reviewed, and topics were found to be distributed as follows:

Conviction of gray marketeer............................2
Arrest/indictment of gray marketeer...............4
Sports bar violations, indictments, settlements...4
Suit against subscribers who returned *modified*
    cable boxes for *repair* (failed the IQ test).....1
Internal investigation of cable company............2
Consumer conviction.....................................1
Managing against cable theft, workshops, etc. ...8
NCTA/COST admin, personalities 2
Incidents involving pirated videotapes.............1
Article on scrambling technology or parts........4

During interviews with cable security specialists, the consensus was that the single most effective weapon against the cable pirate is an angry neighbor or an ex-girlfriend. Most cable companies offer inducements to turn in cable thieves, ranging from bounties to an opportunity to get even. Many who uses modified cable boxes brag that they "get all that stuff for nothing," and when a relationship sours the cable security group is just a phone call away. Most of the country has established state theft-of-service committees, usually made up of representatives of the cable companies. *Secure Signals* published phone numbers of committees that represent about 50% of the national market. They are:

Arizona.............................602-866-0072
California..........................510-372-4300
Colorado...........................303-778-2978
Illinois.............................708-297-4520
Michigan...........................313-540-6733
Minnesota.........................612-483-3233
New England......................617-843-3418
New Jersey........................609-392-3223
New York..........................315-482-9975
West Virginia.....................614-894-6357

There *are* countermeasures against some segments of the cable gray market. Effectiveness depends on the type of equipment in use and the theft methodology. When a cable company's agent purchases a clone, for instance, a technician identifies the coded identity within it, and the system stops transmitting that specific authorization.

One so-called "electronic bullet" countermeasure might be the *de*-authorization of one specific descrambler and all the clones copying its identity. A customer who spent hundreds of dollars to buy a cloned descrambler may find brain-dead junk on his hands. Of course, he can then install, or have installed, a test chip from another category, making his descrambler totally independent of any authorization signal whatsoever.

Other bullets work differently, and require different countermeasures. One is simply DC current that kills every descrambler on the line, including legitimate units that the cable company has decided to replace anyway (usually with a security upgrade). A simple DC block – a common capacitor in series with the signal – is the obvious protection. Some descramblers, on seeing a specific signal on the line (Jerrold, at 106.5 MHz, for instance) will shut down – though this can be prevented by a simple filter trap readily available from gray marketeers. In a few systems, another "bullet" is a specialized instruction that irrevocably turns off the unit unless an ID-specific blocking instruction was previously received and stored. Some modifications may not be designed to store the first signal, so will be rendered inoperable by the second one.

The cable companies can take other steps. According to gray market legend, some premium channels may include a hidden audio signal something like a "cuckoo" clock. That signal is radiated by the cable box or television set at very low power, inaudible on the channel being watched. It is detectable by a receiver in the broadcast FM band, and when a roving agent points his radio's antenna toward a house he can determine whether a TV is tuned to something that shouldn't be available. That signal can sometimes be detected with an FM radio with a SCAN function, like a car radio, when it is reasonably close to the transmitting device. This tactic is likeliest to be used when a highly popular program is being broadcast on one premium channel.

Unless someone reports the cable thief, or his name is given up by a supplier, detection at the consumer level is very unlikely. The economics of the situation make the threat of discovery more apparent than real. Some cable companies let individual cable thieves operate undisturbed, collecting their fees for basic service while they focus their attention on suppliers, because when a supplier is caught his customer list is a perfect trade for leniency. *That's* when the cable company might pay a technician to visit an account and hook up equipment to the cable as it enters the house.

Few modifications to an otherwise legal descrambler can be detected, even with very sophisticated instruments. Gray marketeers advise that such a possibility, however slim, can be eliminated by placing a VCR between the cable's point of entry to the property (where the test instrument would be connected) and the descrambler. Assuming enough time and a skilled operator, test equipment can sometimes estimate how many video components are on the line (though it cannot distinguish between a television set, a VCR, and a descrambler), and the cable company can then reach its own conclusion.

Some cable companies will then write a letter or make a call to the consumer, and using well-chosen words try to motivate the consumer to disconnect the equipment. Of course, that consumer may decide to sell what he believes is no longer safe to use, so the total number of programming thieves may not change. When a consumer is actually caught, however, a fine can result. Some courts have imposed fines based on the assumption that the thief has been stealing services since the first day of cable hookup, and that can be expensive.

The typical consumer-level thief will pay for basic services and steal the rest, but when he must pay for everything he will probably pick only one or two premium services. As mentioned earlier, that might equate to a revenue increase to the cable company of less than $250 per year. When caught, most consumers will add to revenue, but the numbers clearly will not finance a major enforcement effort because so few are detected.

If the consumer has bought his equipment from an out of town source, it obviously cannot be a clone of a local authorized number, and therefore cannot be turned off by a blanket de-authorization signal on the cable. All descrambler modifications sold across state lines use other techniques. If the supplier is caught (and many are, eventually), his records may reflect packages shipped COD to a variety of nationwide addresses – and often to false or useless names. The cable companies and law enforcement agencies are not yet coordinated to pursue any such leads, and not even COST offers an effective way to distribute the information.

There is at least one scenario, however, that can virtually eliminate cable theft. Why some variant of it hasn't been adopted is a mystery...

Step one in the elimination of cable signal theft is the control of unmodified descramblers, which requires the active cooperation of manufacturers, distributors, and the cable companies (who often sell their surplus units to anyone who'll buy it). There is leakage in the supply pipeline between manufacturers, distributors, and the end-user cable companies, so new units flow freely into the gray market, and when a cable company decides to change equipment, the old units are dumped on the open market. Those processes create the very basis of the gray market. After all, how many consumers have the confidence to rip their cable boxes apart and solder a chip in place? Local services to do that would run afoul of state laws, raising their risks. Mail-order services would require the consumer to ship the cable box provided by the cable company to be modified, which he *must* view as a risky procedure. Certainly, therefore, the first step is the control of hardware.

Suppose an agency (COST might be ideal) were to establish a clearing house that lists every legitimate cable company in the country, recording each member's data as to market size and type of scrambling employed. COST would then have a basis by which to approve all sales or transfers of equipment, whether *new* from manufacturers or distributors, or *used* from cable companies who are changing hardware. All members would then be required to get a COST blessing (a transaction number?) before shipping hardware. In fact, it might be economically practical for COST to establish a warehousing facility through which all such hardware transactions pass. Such a facility could be established, equipped, staffed, and operated at a price equal to less than 1% of the cost of programming theft.

Step two requires the adoption of better technology. At least two scrambling/descrambling methodologies seem to be at least expensive – if not impossible – to defeat. One is the Videocipher II+ (for TVRO – see Chapter 1) and the other is the latest Pioneer cable descrambler. Adoption of either of these security strategies (and there may be others as effective) would solve the problem.

So the solution to cable theft is obvious. The industry must control the distribution of hardware, and adopt the best scrambling and security technologies available. The economic forces define the budget for such changes. $480,000,000 per year is more than enough....

The economic equation is very persuasive. Replacing 40,000,000 cable boxes at $50 each equates to a $2 billion investment by the cable industry. If this step eliminates cable theft, within four years the investment will be recovered, and thereafter there will be an additional half billion dollars a year in revenue.

Obstacles to the implementation of such strategies include the narrow view of the cable companies, which seem unwilling to control descrambler logistics, share information, or work together. Some observers believe that the cable companies treat signal theft like shoplifting and insurance fraud, and charge the honest subscriber a fee that takes the estimated theft rate into account. Others believe that cable companies charge advertisers based on a total audience number equal to the sum of paid subscribers plus illegal viewers. There is no fairness in either of these positions.

Combining cable and satellite

Satellite scrambling depends mostly upon confusion and coding of the audio signal; the slightly scrambled video is easily corrected. On the other hand, cable scrambling depends on confusion of the video signal, and the audio signal is not tampered with. Cable companies often receive a satellite signal and instantaneously retransmit it. A consumer with both cable and satellite equipment can use the audio from cable and the video from satellite, and can therefore watch and hear the complete program. Of course, he must still use an illegal gray market "chip" to descramble the video on his satellite receiver, but since most cable scrambling techniques distort only the video, the audio from the cable channel will be loud and clear.

There may well be delay (sometimes half a second, sometimes... *days*) between the two signals, requiring complex mixing of satellite video and cable audio to produce a viewable result. Though something of a hobby to its practitioners, technically it is still theft.

The United States Criminal Code prohibits the broadcast of information concerning "any lottery, gift enterprise, or similar scheme."

Federal Communications Commission Information Bulletin 4/88

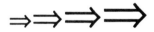

LOTTERY RESULTS

**Saturday, 8:00PM
Channel 5**

*TV Guide
almost any city...*

VIDEOTAPE

Why copy protection?

The entertainment industry became upset about the ease with which a consumer can copy a rented videotape, and went to the technologists for a solution. They got one – and the solution has created a small industry of measures and countermeasures, products and counterproducts.

Today's videotape production houses bury a specialized signal in the video that causes few problems in a television set but overloads a critical process that occurs only in a typical video recorder. Technically, the protection method hides a high-level signal within a certain space in the video, high enough to cause a problem when combined with the VCR's recording process but usually just low enough to avoid distorting the image on a television set. Known as EIDAK™, Copyguard™ and Macrovision™, these products and techniques are firmly established in the video marketplace.

EIDAK™ by MIT changes video signal timing and adds multiple stripes to the recorded signal. Macrovision™ puts five white pulses in the vertical blanking interval, tricking the VCR's automatic gain control circuitry into thinking there is an overload input signal, producing a loss of color and other visual defects. Copyguard™ is similar.

The "video stabilizer"

Copy protection systems work well, but the "few problems" created a gray market opportunity. Perhaps the same companies and individuals that devised the copy protection techniques also funded or worked on consumer "video stabilization" devices that *remove* the copy protection.

"Video copy protection removers," "video stabilizers," and "video enhancers" are all generally the same thing, and are naively sold by highly ethical stores and mail order businesses. Nearly all are specifically designed to reverse the copy protection process. There is one exception – some "video enhancers" actually reduce distortion and improve color. It's easy to tell the difference by looking at the vendor's claims. Many products are sold with accompanying explicit statements that states they're "designed to remove Copyguard™ and Macrovision™ and permit duplication of videotapes."

That's *very* clear, indeed. The manufacturer and the retailer are selling tools, the primary function of which is the violation of copyright law.

Industry countermeasures and consumer risk

It is unlikely that the purchaser of a "video stabilizer" would be subject to a household search warrant (!). Neither the entertainment industry nor law enforcement agencies have plans or resources to track down copyright violators, though they easily could by forcing the production of purchaser records from the large group of manufacturers and retailers.

One way for a consumer to get in serious trouble is to start a cottage industry. He could rent a number of videotapes, buy packages, color-xerox the labels, use a stabilizer to produce good copies, and then set up a booth at a flea market. Many such cottage industries openly sell pirated video and audio tapes at swap meets and flea markets around the country. Even this blatant violation, however, is difficult to police.

Some people sell hard-core pornography videos, copied from an original, knowing that the porn industry does a poor job of policing. Major newspapers of many cities run the same classified ads every day, for "HARD-CORE

XXX VIDEOS, ONLY $8 EACH." It's easy to sell profitably at such a price when blank tape costs less than $2 in quantity, and no royalties are paid.

Unless there are plans to start such a cottage industry, the consumer can rent a movie once and, with a video stabilizer, make a copy for a personal library or to give to a friend – all without great fear that the front door will come crashing down.

"Problem one is piracy – the theft of American movie products. When you make something that most people want to see, someone is going to steal it."

Jack Valenti
President
Motion Picture Association of America
1991

as reported in *Secure Signals*

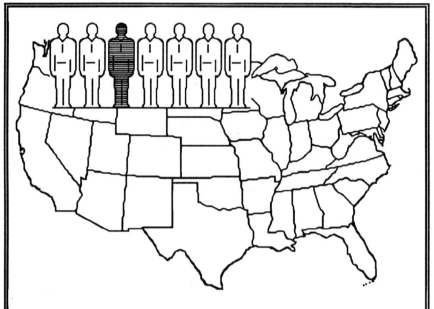

...answers to the question: "How many cheat?"

"7%" (TCI of Dallas)
"We lose one dollar in five" (CA Cable TV executive)
"One in ten" (cable company security manager)
"Most" (consumer justifying his modified descrambler)
"Everyone who knows how" (chip vendor)
"Very few – maybe 1%" ("innocent" consumer)
"We get no complaints at all" (local police sergeant)

SELLERS & BUYERS

Gray market wheelers and dealers

What converts an honest businessman into a member of the gray market? As one would expect, it's money, because the profits can be quite remarkable and risk is not perceived as high. A $60,000,000 annual market (and that's cable only!) is a huge pie, so even a narrow slice is big. Within that gray market are many diverse opportunities to convert knowledge, access, and effort into illegal profits. The price differential between legitimate and gray market sales places high pressure within the legitimate supply pipeline, and causes leaks of both information and hardware.

A wholesaler/distributor might charge a cable company one-fifth of the price advertised by those who *"absolutely, positively, cannot ship to customers in the state of _____."* The gray market mark-up is enormous.

A descrambler with a distributor price of $40 might be worth $300 or more to a consumer once it's been modified. A few hours of programming effort can produce disks that can be sold to chip programmers for hundreds of dollars each. A programming instrument can produce hundreds of descrambling chips per day, and a memory chip that retails for $1 unprogrammed is worth between $10 and $50 with the software on it.

The legitimate descrambler supply line for cable equipment is vulnerable at several points, and financial pressure can cause it to leak both information and hardware. One gray market vendor might be a descrambler distributor who is financing his survival through the recession by shipping a few hundred extra units to an out-of-state gray marketeer. An insider in the cable equipment business might "leak" technical information. An engineer or programmer might take on "consulting" tasks to write software to be embedded in chips to be sold by others. With such software, almost anyone can use a programming instrument to turn out chips by the hundreds.

These suppliers are "professionals" at the heart of the gray market, and are – and should be – primary targets of the enforcement agencies. There are also many amateurs in this business, however. If there is insufficient reason or resources to go after the professionals, what risk does the amateur face?

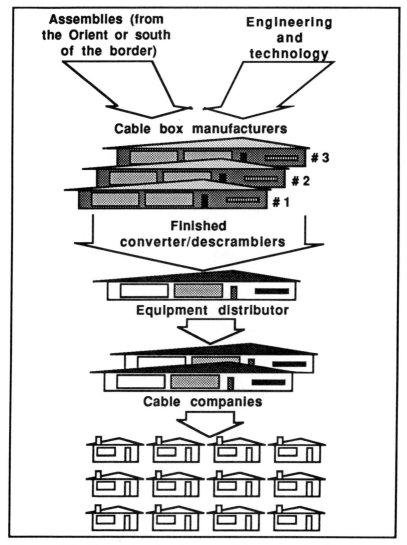

Figure 11: Legitimate descrambler supply line.

Even an untrained consumer might buy a chip for his own cable box, learn how to install it, and then buy a dozen cable boxes and chips to convert them, and sell the result at a swap meet or to friends and neighbors. Even simpler, such a "civilian" could do a deal with a national mail-order vendor of complete modified descramblers, packaged as new equipment in the original carton, and act as a local "sales representative." College students have financed their education in this business – and some have stayed in it.

After a while, paranoia fades, the revenue stops feeling "extra," and the operation is rationalized until it feels reasonably honest and safe. It is neither. If they sell within their own state, those gray marketeers risk prosecution by local law enforcement agencies, or lawsuits by cable companies.

From a risk standpoint, a gray marketeer is far safer in dealing exclusively with out-of-state customers. There are federal laws against theft of programming, but they're enforced by non-criminal actions in civil courts, or by busy federal agencies that have higher priorities. To gray market vendors working with national customers, there is probably more risk of an IRS investigation than a confrontation with law enforcement agencies.

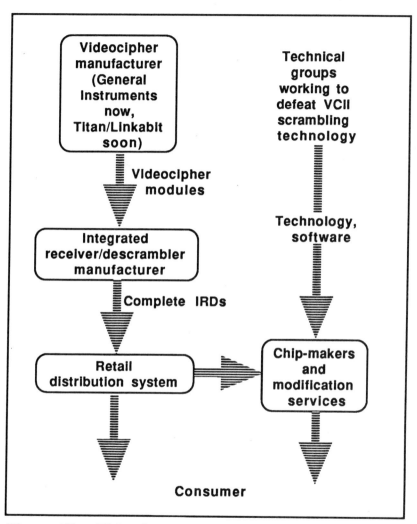

Figure 12: Videocipher supply lines, gray and otherwise.

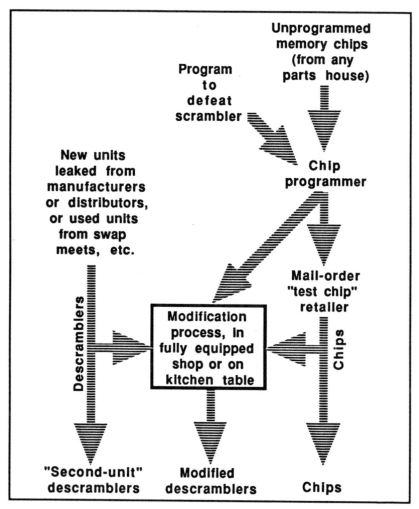

Figure 13: The gray supply line for cable descramblers.

Advertising, and finding customers, is easy. Major retailers buy full page ads for "...second-unit descramblers. You must sign a statement that you are a full subscriber or...". Periodicals with otherwise very high standards are happy to accept such advertising, and ads that are far more candid and suggestive are printed by many magazines: ads such as *"Our modified descramblers provide full service...", or "This test chip even works on Pay-Per-View!"* leave little doubt.

Almost anyone might buy an illegal descrambler, and the business end of this gray market also covers the spectrum of our economy and society. It includes highly-trained technologists who "reverse engineer" a new descrambler and write software to defeat it, distributors of chips and cable boxes, retailers of such "test devices" and modified descramblers, local sales reps, kitchen-table technicians, college students, and out-of-work carpenters. It's hard to be hypercritical of someone who accepts the risk of getting caught to avoid seeing his home go back to the bank.

It's easy, however, to find fault with those who simply view programming theft as another business opportunity, and many of the participants in the gray market are in precisely that category.

Whether a wholesaler/distributor who siphons off a few units to sell at grossly inflated prices, an engineer who takes a few extra dollars to develop a descrambling chip "on the side," a housewife who helps her neighbors get more for their cable company check, or a cold-hearted businessman who writes an operating plan, invests, and sets up a solid (but illegal) business, these people are subject to both local and federal laws and penalties. Is it worth the risk? Some wink at the law or believe there is no risk whatsoever, and act accordingly.

They're wrong. There is risk to *every* level of gray market activity, from the technician who lets slip a "back door" to a descrambler program to a multi-million-dollar retailer. And, of course, there's risk to the end-user because that retailer has only his customer list to trade when he's plea-bargaining.

Conversations with dealers

In all cases, the caller identified himself as an author and described this book and its purpose. The following discussion is a "composite" of four interviews, but except for minor grammatical changes and the removal of expletives or potentially identifying material, the dialogs are reported verbatim. The dealers were selected by picking advertisements that listed no location or company name. After establishing the author's identity and purpose, and developing a certain rapport, the first serious question was always the same: *"Can I record this conversation?"* Here is what followed:

A. *If you don't use my name, maybe. What kind of questions do you want to ask?*

Q. *About your business, who you sell to and buy from. The risk. That sort of thing.*

A. *I don't want to be identified.*

Q. *You won't be. I've called a lot of numbers trying to find someone who'll talk with me, and I've lost my place on the page, so I'm not even sure what your number is. Besides, I'm only calling ads with no company name.*

A. *Yeah. Ok. Go ahead and record this. But wait, will you keep the tape?*

Q. *Is that a problem?*

A. *Yeah. I want a promise the tape will be erased so no one can hear my voice. Will you talk about this in your book?*

Q. *I want to, and I promise the tape will be destroyed. I'll make a verbatim transcript, but in the book what you say will be integrated with the comments from other dealers. I mean, the book will contain a mixture of your ideas and those of others. Now, can I record this conversation or not?*

A. *OK. Go ahead. Let's keep it short, OK?*

Q. *Sure. How long have you been in business?*

A. *About a year. I worked for my dad before that, doing the same thing but for satellite instead of cable. We did Videociphers, and before that Sony. Does your book talk about satellite, too?*

Q. *Yes, but cable is the most important topic. Did your satellite business make money?*

A. *Absolutely, at least until last year. We had two new cars, and we lived pretty good. The new descramblers are a bitch, so we had to buy the old style modules on the black market for a lot of money, and our margin shrunk. He's still doing it, though.*

Q. *Why did you stop working for him?*

A. *It seemed like time to move out on my own. I'm doing pretty well in cable, you know.*

Q. *Do you advertise anywhere but Nuts & Volts? Just how do you find customers?*

A. *Yeah. That only works for the people who are already looking, though. To start people thinking I put notices on supermarket bulletin boards, too, but my local advertising is for a friend who's out of state, and he does the same for me in his area. It works out about even, I guess. I don't deal locally. Never.*

My best customers are old customers. They go into business for themselves, with their friends. You know what multi-level marketing is? That's what I'm doing, but it's not like Amway. I'm at the top.

Q. *You mean your customers sell to others who sell to others, and so forth?*

A. *Make one new customer happy and soon you've got five or ten units a month going to that same person or at least to that same neighborhood in the same town. They trickle down. That's not what the Republicans are talking about, though.*

Q. *In the last year, how many units have you shipped?*

A. *Boxes or chips? Boxes... I guess a couple hundred. Chips... maybe a few more. Some of my customers have gone into business for themselves. And I sell to some stores, too. Did you know they're putting chips in boxes on the repair bench? It doesn't take much.*

Q. *Hold on. One question at a time. Where do you get the chips? They're the key, right? I mean, you have to have the chips before you can sell anything at all.*

A. *I make the chips – actually, I get someone to make them for me. He doesn't know what they're all about, though. He's just a chip duplication service. What I did was buy a chip and get him to read the code and start programming others like that. It didn't work for everything. Some of the chips have what they call a fusible link, where after they're done programming it you can't read what's in it. I bought some software for chips that have that problem, and it works fine.*

Q. *What's a chip worth?*

A. *Nothing until the right program is on it. Once that's done, it's worth whatever I can get for it. Maybe $25 most of the time. It depends. If the customer saw an ad, then the price is low because there's lots of ads and lots of dealers and lots of prices. If "Joe sent me," you know, the price can go up because the customer knows* *it's safe, you know. My best deals are referrals. You know, from satisfied clients. Don't sell a chip to a guy unless he knows what to do with it. I did a little instruction sheet. That helps.*

Q. *How many different boxes do you sell? And where do you get them? That must be a problem. I mean finding a reliable source.*

A. *At first only Zenith, but I'll take orders for anything now. Anything. Some boxes I get from a company that siphons them from a distributor. New ones, and I pay a lot for them. Maybe a lot more than it ought to be, but there's a lot of room in the prices so who cares?*

Q. *I see a lot of new units advertised by legitimate distributors, and the prices don't seem too bad. Why do you think they're high?*

A. *Legitimate? The only legitimate customer for a distributor is a cable company, and the only legitimate place for a consumer to get a box is the cable company. Anything outside that isn't legitimate, and the prices show it. You know. They're high, but what can you do?*

Q. *What about used ones? I see ads offering to buy used units.*

A. *Sometimes I'll buy used ones at a garage sale or swap meet for a few dollars. There's a property manager in (deleted) who handles hundreds of apartments, and we have a deal for abandoned cable boxes. Used isn't bad. You can get a new remote for a few bucks, stick a couple bucks worth of chip inside, wipe it off, and then get $200 for it. Maybe more. That's what makes this so profitable.*

Also, if someone calls for something I don't have there's people I can call. You can't call a customer back, though, so I say it's right here and ready to go, and then after I take the order I'll call around to find what the customer wants.

Q. *How's business? And where's it the best?*

A. *Business is great. I ship a lot to the west coast. I work with a guy in L.A. who can't ship to local customers but they're crawling all over him, so I meet the need and we work it out. He sends me descramblers, too. I guess California is my best market. Where are you calling from?*

Q. *(answer deleted) Do you do any business here?*

A. *Everywhere. Everywhere. Would you believe I'm helping the trade balance? We actually ship to the borders, and the boxes make it into both Canada and Mexico. I think. Anyway, I just sent a hundred chips to an address in San Ysidro. That's on the border with Mexico, right? Where do you think they'll go?*

Q. *I see a lot of ads like yours, and there's no secrecy about what you're advertising. What's the risk the authorities will get after you?*

A. *Zero point zero. They might go after some of the bigger guys, I guess. Why should they mess with me when it takes the same effort to go after someone ten times my size? And they actually don't go after very many. I hear about busts. Most of them. There isn't much trouble. At least near here.*

Q. *Who enforces the law?*

A. *If you deal locally you can get in trouble from the cable company and the police. You know, the city police. That's what I understand. I got a lawyer. Can you believe that? A lawyer! She told me to keep my business outside the state because the locals are a lot more likely to hassle me than the feds.*

Q. *Can you count on her advice?*

A. *She's got more than just me. I mean she represents a couple of others in the same business. That's how I got referred to her, by a friend. She's pretty smart. She'll call me now and then, and I think she calls others, talks to them, even to other attorneys. So her information comes from a lot of people and a lot of sources. Yeah, I count on her advice. I believe it.*

Q. *So you don't have much of a threat. What if I buy a cable box from you. What's the risk to me?*

A. *Where do you live?*

Q. *(answer deleted)*

A. *I never heard of any trouble there. I've heard of people who have been using chipped boxes for a long time, and not one word of trouble. One guy in your town had a mono Zenith and wanted a stereo one. He sold his old one for more than I charged him for a new one. I hear about trouble sometimes, but it's the news, not the fact. Know what I mean?*

Q. *No. What do you mean by that?*

A. *There's more news about prosecution than there really is prosecution. And more rumors. Actually, there's not much going on out there. It's pretty safe, I*

*think. At least, my competition thinks so. This is a
very big market. If there is trouble, we all hear about
it. It's pretty quiet. Even though there's a problem
somewhere, that doesn't mean there's trouble a few
miles further down the road, you know? It's a big
country. Every cable company is on its own. They
could get together, I guess, but they don't.*

Q. *If I bought a unit, what's the chance that someone
will come banging on my door?*

A. *No guarantees. But how will they know which door
to bang on? I won't tell them.*

Q. *What if you were arrested? Wouldn't you give up
my name and so forth to help your situation?*

A. *No. You're safe. I'd protect my customers.*

(Pause while interviewer recovered from coughing fit)

Q. *But what if they do catch me? What happens?*

A. *Maybe they'd take you to court, but I hear they'll
just make threats and then ask for money to cover their
losses. I mean, they might figure that you've had full
service since the system was hooked up, and only paid
for basic, right? And want you to pay the difference.*

That could be thousands. I wouldn't worry much, though. They're too busy making money to worry about missing a few.

Q. *How do you ship to your customers?*

A. *Usually UPS. Sometimes I've sent things on Greyhound, especially if it's just to _____ (a city across the state line). That's only an hour or so. Funny, everyone's in a hurry. It might take three phone calls to make a decision, but then it's <u>right now</u>.*

Q. *How do you get paid?*

A. *Money orders, checks, cash, COD. Cash. Some people actually send me cash. Once I get to know one of my multi-level customers maybe I'll ship by bus and he'll pay with a personal check. We trust each other. How can you do business if you can't trust each other? (Laughs)*

Q. *I mean new customers. Do you take credit cards? How do you handle the transaction?*

A. *Well, no. I don't take credit cards. This isn't K-Mart. (Laughs) Someone calls... The customer calls, and if we do a deal he'll give me his address and*

I'll ship COD, or he'll send me a money order. You know, to my post office box. COD is better, though.

Q. *Aren't you worried that the next phone call will be the police, trying to get you to incriminate yourself?*

A. *That would be a first. And what would they do? I haven't broken any state laws.*

Q. *Is your business growing?*

A. *Nope. This is about the right size. It pays the bills and I don't think there's much risk unless I get bigger.*

Q. *Is this your only income?*

A. *No. I work full time. This just takes a few hours a week. Actually, my wife mostly sticks the chips in. Actually, she works harder at this than I do. We share it. I'm the president of this company and she's the labor force. (Laughs) Management and labor...*

Q. *You work full time. What do you do?*

A. *I'm a marshal. You know, that's not a cop. It's not like Marshal Dillon. We serve papers – escort prisoners – that sort of thing. I'm a marshal.*

Who enforces the law?

After many tries, the author finally connected with the police or sheriff departments in three towns or cities where gray market companies are situated, and where those companies' unambiguous advertisements included their name and address. He talked with either a desk sergeant or a spokesperson, explained the subject of the book, and established his credibility. It was difficult.

The interviewer tried to keep the conversation very casual, saying "this isn't for the record. No, I'm just collecting background." Once the serious questions began, no single conversation lasted more than three minutes. The following is a composite report, but is close to verbatim. No recording was made because it would have prevented open discussion. The questions were prepared in advance, and notes were made of the responses. Note: the purpose of the book and of the conversation was firmly established before the questions were asked.

Q. *This is about companies that sell modified cable descramblers, right? I want to know whether they're violating any of the laws enforced by your department?*

A. *Probably not. I've been asked this before. Isn't that federal or something? We've got other fish to fry.*

Q. *Who asked you this question before?*

A. *Guys going into the business? (Laugh) I don't know. Nothing official. Maybe another writer?*

Q. *If you knew, that _____ (naming a company), at _____ (that company's address), was modifying descramblers and selling them to consumers who steal programming, what would you do about it?*

A. *What was that address? (Laugh) No, really. No, I just do what I do. The job. Which is pretty much to keep the streets safe. That other guy is the postal inspector's problem, right? Or something like that. It might be a crime somewhere, but not on our books.*

Q. *What do you think of a guy that sets up such a business? You know, he gets around the law and cheats the cable companies out of their lawful revenue? Don't you want to do something about it?*

A. *You've never been a cop, that's for sure. That stuff is for lawsuits, not the police. It's copyright violation, right? We're loaded with perps who use knives and guns. That's what gets my attention.*

The author then put on his paranoia shield and went to a payphone to call the local Federal Building. When connected with an agent of the FBI, the author attempted to begin the dialog as described above.

The agent said that the situation mentioned was potentially in violation of federal law, and he asked for further details. He was like a steel sponge – he soaked up information but didn't answer one question during a two minute conversation.

The author is a reasonably competent interviewer, but in this case was unable to elicit any meaningful information whatever regarding FBI interest in, or enforcement of, any laws governing the manufacture or sale of devices designed/produced to permit theft of programming.

Who buys these products and services?

How can you describe the gray market customer? Few of us are perfectly honest all the time. At least occasionally, virtually all of us ignore the speed limit, add a few dollars to certain columns in our tax return, pad an expense account, or fail to tell the clerk that the bill should be $10 higher. These acts all violate either the law or ethics, but which are criminal?

> ## FINANCIAL PRESSURE ON THE CONSUMER
>
> Typical cost of legitimate
> service for one year .... $500 - 1,000
>
> *VERSUS*
>
> Cost of illegal descrambler $250
>
> *OR*
>
> Cost of "test device" for consumer
> able to install it himself $25
>
> *THEREFORE*
>
> **Five year savings .... $2,475 - $4,975**

In the television gray market, there's light gray and dark gray, and a well-meaning and basically honest citizen can find it easy to move in small steps from the entry to the dark end. For instance, he might begin by illegally copying a videotape so his spouse can see the program at a more convenient time (you *do* read the warning that precedes the movie, don't you?). To improve the result, he can buy a $50 "stabilizer," advertised in his favorite magazine and sold by some of our most respected retailers. That's already past white and into gray, but is he a criminal yet?

Our "honest citizen" reads *OMNI, Sporting News, Popular Mechanics*, and a host of other first-rate periodicals that happen to include descrambler advertising, and over time he correlates that information with the recollection that he "rents" his descrambler from the cable company. He might therefore buy a unit, disregarding or forgetting his contractual obligation to use only the cable company's equipment. Of course, he will then add an outlet in his home, and must seek the tools and parts and skill to do that. He becomes aware of other gray market opportunities and becomes expert at rationalizing what he's already done. Finally, when he (1) considers "the inflated price of programming," and (2) spots a suggestive ad for a "test device," he might be stimulated to accept increased criminality – and liability.

Whether he begins with a TVRO installation or a cable contract, the end result of this process is theft of programming, which the consumer knows (or should know) is punishable by law. On the other hand, rationalization and advertising keep every step as easy as the previous one. The risk is perceived as very low because, as the consumer becomes aware of the market, he sees more and more blatant activity. What could be more clear than an advertisement that says "Our 'test chip' restores your cable box to full service. See even Pay-Per-View programming." The consumer steals services, becomes tolerant of the perceived risk, grows conversant in the terminology of the gray market, and grooms himself for the next step.

The most serious transition would be a move into the gray market as an active participant, when the consumer begins selling modified cable boxes to his friends. It's at that point that enforcement groups begin looking for him, and penalties can be high. They are reduced, of course, when that supplier cooperates by providing the enforcers with a list of customer names...

Who is the programming thief? If the steps from white to dark gray are kept small, and the risk is not obvious, it can be almost anyone.

Conversation with a gray market consumer (turned dealer)

The author was unable to contact a single-unit customer who would permit a discussion. After several attempts, one conversation was made possible by a dealer who convinced a customer who had turned into a multi-level-marketeer to call the author. The caller was unwilling to have the call recorded, and after preliminaries the following is a paraphrase of the result, taken from notes.

Q. *In what part of the country do you live?*

A. *Southern California.*

Q. *How long have you used a modified cable box?*

A. *Two years.*

Q. *What got you started?*

A. *At a swap meet I bought a cable box just like the one the cable company had given me. I added cable and connectors and had a second outlet at no cost, and it got HBO. I didn't understand that, so I started asking around and the answers got me looking at magazines, the classified section.*

Q. *What did you find?*

A. *A lot of people cheat, and it's easy to do. It doesn't cost much, and there doesn't appear to be any risk. I just ordered what I wanted from an ad, COD.*

Q. *What about risk?*

A. *I can only speak about my area, but I've probably sold a hundred boxes and I've never heard of anyone having a problem.*

Q. *So you're a dealer?*

A. *Yes. I started by telling a friend that I could get him a box like mine. He's a dealer now, and he works for me. I've got four like him, and each one does a couple of boxes a month.*

Q. *How much money do you make?*

A. *I keep about $25-30 a box, so that's close to $300 a month extra for me. I don't sell to the end user any more, I'm a sort of wholesaler with zero overhead, so the additional income is all profit.*

Q. *How much money do your associates keep?*

A. *We've talked about it, and it's more. If there is risk, they take more of it than I do. I'm like a wholesaler. I don't talk with the customers.*

Q. *How do they find business?*

A. *100% word of mouth. If it works for someone, there will be someone he trusts enough to tell.*

Q. *What would happen if the authorities caught you?*

A. *I don't know. But I don't think they're looking. I believe the worst risk is that someone will get in an argument with someone who's using an illegal box, and will call the cable company and report him.*

Q. *Does the cable company offer a bounty?*

A. *I've never heard of it if they do.*

Q. *Do you need to be technically competent to be a local distributor?*

A. *No. The first boxes had some switches on them that had to be set. Once we learned the correct setting the rest were put together with no switches. The settings are wired inside the box.*

Q. *How many switches?*

A. *Two. Not very complicated.*

Q. *How well do the boxes work?*

A. *The same as the units from the cable company. And the customer gets a 100% guarantee.*

Q. *What if a box breaks?*

A. *I'll replace it if I have a spare, and I usually keep one. It will go back to my supplier, who'll fix it free.*

Q. *How much do you pay for a box as a distributor?*

A. *I'd rather not say.*

Q. *What prevents your salesmen from finding their own sources and cutting you out?*

A. *I don't know. They haven't, though, so they must not be looking very hard. Suppliers are easy to find. This whole thing works, and I don't keep much, so maybe they don't have reason to.*

Q. *Do you have a conflict with the ethics of this?*

A. *I did. I'm a churchgoer and basically honest. I don't now. After all, we know the cable is ripping us off, and that makes it easier. Also, there's not really any threat. If this were serious stuff, there would be.*

Q. *What's your primary line of work?*

A. *I'm a salesman in (a large retail store chain).*

Consumers and the dark gray process

What exactly does the gray market consumer do once he's decided to steal programming? When financial pressure (or simply greed) has pushed him past the morality obstacle, and he's rationalized that the programmers are overcharging and "everyone's doing it," he need only pick up the phone and place his order. The industry has made it very simple for the consumer to buy an illegally modified descrambler.

Based upon whether the system is cable or TVRO, a reasonably credible vendor is selected from ads that offer "test devices" and descramblers. Such vendors, it may be assumed, not only sell "chips" that enable the consumer to modify his own unit, but also sell complete descramblers in which the required chip has been installed with reasonable competence.

How does that consumer further qualify the vendor? One of the safest ways is to select one that offers credit card services, since credit card transactions usually provide recourse. He will, of course, use a vendor outside his own state, though the 800-number makes it difficult to determine the location of the retailer. It makes sense to select a vendor who includes an address in his advertising. If a catalog is offered by mail, and the vendor fails to perform, there may be recourse through postal authorities. A physical address (not a post office box) adds substance to the vendor and increases the likelihood that the consumer is dealing with an established retailer rather than a highly transient kitchen table operation.

As of mid-1992, for a modified satellite descrambler the consumer will probably pay between $300 and $500, and for a modified cable box the price might range from $250 to $350 (depending on the brand).

The technically competent buyer can simply purchase the required unmodified units plus chips (or "test devices") at some price between $10 to $200, but that option is risky because the dealer may blame the buyer's workmanship if the result doesn't operate as expected.

The cautious consumer, therefore, will usually purchase a *completely modified unit* from an out-of-state and catalog-mailing retailer who accepts payment by credit card. On the other hand, the more reputable the dealer the likelier he'll keep customer records, and when his door comes crashing down the only asset he can deal with is his customer list. How can the consumer's risk be eliminated? It cannot, if a credit card is used, because it's a relatively simple process (with subpoena in hand) for a law enforcement agency to identify customers.

Amazingly, reports indicate that most gray market
dealers offer guarantees – and *honor* them. If a
modified descrambler fails, and some do, a warranty is
likely to be valid. Not all are, and many companies go
into and out of business with remarkable ease (witness
the suppliers who advertise without listing a company
name – the ad includes only a "test chip" claim and
phone number). It's not possible, of course, to take a
modified descrambler to your local cable company for
service. Even owning a gray market *un*modified unit
violates the terms of most cable company contracts.

The wary consumer, bent on stealing programming,
must accept one risk or another. The vendor may ship
non-working junk and then disappear, he may float
away with no way to ever find him if the descrambler
breaks, or the vendor might trade his customer list for
leniency if/when he is arrested.

Is there a safe way the consumer can guarantee the
desired result? There is not. The modification may
work when delivered, and may work for some period,
but it can – and probably will – succumb to one
countermeasure or another, and then re-modifying the
descrambler can become increasingly costly. Finally,
there is no way the consumer can guarantee that his
cable company will never learn his name...
and his game.

THE MEDIA

Popular periodicals

The print medium that supports the television gray market is divided into three general categories. The first is advertising in the "popular" press, where the publisher addresses a conventional market but permits (and perhaps solicits) advertising from gray marketeers. Some periodicals in this category include:

Popular Science	*Car & Driver*
Popular Mechanics	*TV Guide*
Popular Electronics	*Omni*
Video Magazine	*Sporting News*
Video Review	*National Inquirer*

and many, many others that focus upon automobiles, hobbies, sports, etc.

Obviously, these magazines enjoy wide circulation and are editorially above reproach. The reader may ask why they carry advertisements for products that (1) can only be sold to out of state customers and (2) assist the consumer who seeks to violate his contract with his cable company.

Gray market focus

A second category preaches to the choir, and includes advertising and editorial material that addresses aspects of the electronics gray market, including television, scanning, automotive electronics, privacy violation, etc. Among others, this category includes:

Nuts & Volts	800-783-4624
Popular Communications	516-681-2922
Radio Electronics Magazine	516-293-3000
Popular Electronics	516-293-3000
Scrambling News	1552 Hertel Ave
	Buffalo, NY 14216

Specialized pamphlets, manuals, etc.

The third category is made up of non-periodic booklets or pamphlets on television gray market issues.

Cable Facts (Adams Cable Service) was copyrighted in 1982, but certain dated content indicates at least a partial rewrite. In seventeen pages, this pamphlet does a good though somewhat archaic job of explaining how cable systems are/were intended to work, and describes simple traps and reverse traps that block or confuse some premium channels. $9.95.

Cable TV Equipment List 1992 is advertised as a "secret" list of cable equipment dealers and costs $15.99. It provides a total of thirty-eight entries including "JEROLD (*sic*) EQUIPMENT SALES, INC." The "secret" list ends with an ad for a $19.99 list of government auctions, and includes a one-page flyer that offers to add the name of any dealer to the list for only $15. *Silly.*

The VCR/Cable TV Survival Guide, by Harshman, is $10.95. It's a consumer-level description of cable TV and VCR operation, though it is not superior to many similarly priced books available in bookstores. *Competent.*

By far the most literate publication in the *gray* market is a newsletter called *Scrambling News*. It seems to be complete, timely, and accurate. It includes excellent coverage of legislation, corporate relations in the scrambling industries, and business intentions. *Interesting and recommended.*

"Broadcast stations are licensed to serve the public convenience, interest, and necessity."

Federal Communications Commission

"I can't afford the cable bill, and in my family the programming is a necessity."

...a programming thief

GLOSSARY

The television gray market has a vocabulary of its own. This glossary is far from complete, as new vernacular evolves regularly. It is sufficient, however, to assist the reader who seeks to interpret an advertisement or article on the subjects of cable or satellite television.

ADDRESSABLE DESCRAMBLER
A converter/descrambler that contains its own electronic identity and can therefore receive messages from the cable company, including those which turn ON and OFF the descrambling circuit.

AUDIO CODE
The special code that the authorization process sends to a Videocipher to permit descrambling of the audio. Available by dialing 900-SUMMONS, where for $3.50 a tape recorded message will relate the numbers required to authorize a descrambler for a month of premium channel audio (descrambling satellite *video* is a trivial task).

BACK DOOR
Entry to a software program provided by the engineer/programmer to permit patches and later changes without having to cross password barriers.

BRAIN-DEAD

The result of a Videocipher losing its internal battery, or receiving a "die" command from the satellite. Once brain dead, the descrambler (applies to cable, also) is useless unless/until it is illegally programmed to a new identity by a cloning process.

BULLET (1)

Usually a de-authorization signal sent by the cable company once the identity of a clone is discovered, thus turning off all units with that identity; applies equally to Videocipher and cable boxes.

BULLET (2)

Often DC (direct current) sent down the cable line feeding a block of customers, which burns out the input stage of *all* descramblers unless the current is blocked by a capacitor in series with the cable. Of course, only legitimate units are then repaired. More sophisticated digital "bullets" exist, also.

CABLE (1)

A wired television distribution system (colloquial).

CABLE (2)

The shielded wire between the TV and the head end, usually designated RG-58 or 59 – printed on the cable itself.

CABLE (3)
The programming emanating from a cable-based system, differentiated from OFF-AIR.

CATV
Community Antenna TeleVision. Originally, one antenna plus amplification and distribution cables. Now this term is used in apartments, etc., to denote one *cable* input, distributed to all subscribers or residents, often with one subscription payment.

CHANNEL
In television parlance, a simple numeric designator of a frequency on which a television channel is broadcast. Across the country, all stations that transmit on Channel 7 use the same frequency band (174 to 180 MHz), which is why any TV set can operate anywhere in the country.

CHIP (1)
As a noun, an integrated circuit that either contains memory capacity with a descrambling instruction or a microprocessor (computer) that is capable of fooling other circuitry into descrambling unsubscribed programming.

CHIP (2)
>   As a verb, to install a semiconductor integrated circuit into a descrambler such as to make the unit descramble unsubscribed programming.

CHIPPED
>   Colloquially, a cable or TVRO descrambler that has been modified, as in "this box is chipped."

CLONE
>   A descrambler, for cable or satellite, in which the identity of another (usually fully subscribed) unit has been embedded.

CONVERTER
>   An active electrical circuit that converts the cable frequencies to a new frequency that can be tuned by a television set (usually channel 3 or 4). Some "cable ready" television sets are equipped with circuitry to do that conversion internally, but that does not solve the scrambling problem.

CRACKING TOOL
>   To some, a specialized tool required to open a sealed cable box or Videocipher module.

CUCKOO

An audio signal impressed on a radio-frequency carrier, which is then radiated by the TV set or the descrambler at a very low level. A proper antenna and radio combination, aimed at the radiating unit, can detect a signal which, when demodulated, produces an audible "CUCKOO" sound. This identifies which homes are viewing the affected channels. This signal is usually added to popular Pay-Per-View programming, but in some markets may appear on any premium channel.

DBS

The Direct Broadcast Satellite will permit viewing many channels without need of a dish. A flat "phased array" antenna can be installed on a window and simply wired to a specialized receiver (with an integrated descrambler, of course). DBS transmits at a higher power level than conventional satellite TV transponders, hence the small antenna.

DES

Digital Encryption Standard, developed by the National Security Agency and adopted by the Videocipher as an uncrackable coding method. It was the usage of DES software that generated a futile Department of Commerce edict forbidding export of the Videocipher.

DESCRAMBLER
Virtually always packaged *with* a converter, the descrambler restores to the video signal all data removed or distorted by the scrambling process, so a conventional TV can operate properly.

DISH
In the context of consumer television broadcasting, a circular concave assembly from 4' to 12', aimed at the appropriate satellite, which focuses the radio energy from the satellite onto an amplifier at the focal point of the dish. The dish is moved along the arc on which the satellites are located by a motor.

DOWNLINK
The signal path *from* the transponder *to* the earth.

EPOXY (also POTTING)
A two-part coating used to restrict access to critical circuitry in some early Videocipher descramblers. Easily dissolved or ground away.

FEDERAL COMMUNICATIONS COMMISSION
The FCC is responsible for allocation of the radio spectrum and management of its use. It assigns frequency limits and power limits to everything that broadcasts radio energy, from TV stations to walkie-talkies. It polices usage and can levy fines, confiscate goods, and file federal criminal charges.

FEED (1)
The device at the focal point of a dish antenna, where the energy is focused and converted into a form usable by the receiver (indoors).

FEED (2)
Newscast or other program segment from a remote site to the studio, often by mobile satellite (truck-mounted antenna). Sporting events, political rallies, etc. are all passed to the studio by a FEED. Many TVRO owners enjoy scanning transponders looking for unedited and commercial-free feeds.

FILTER
A circuit that passes frequencies selectively. Some self-destruct after a prescribed period.

FILTER (BAND-PASS, OR BPF)
A filter that passes every frequency that is *above* one frequency and *below* a second, and blocks all others.

FILTER (HIGH-PASS, OR HPF)
A filter that passes all frequencies *above* a specified frequency, blocking those that are lower.

FILTER (LOW-PASS, OR LPF)
A filter that passes all frequencies *below* a specified frequency, blocking those that are higher.

FILTER (NOTCH)
A filter that removes a portion of the signal, such as a reverse band-pass filter, and passes the rest of the signal unaltered.

GATED PULSE
One scrambling technique, by which a precise pulse is introduced to suppress a critical part of the video signal.

GEOSTATIONARY
Term used to describe satellites that are in an orbit that keeps them precisely over one point on the earth. That occurs at about 22,500 miles from the surface.

GI
General Instruments, in San Diego, manufacturer of the Videocipher (TVRO descrambler) and Jerrold (cable descrambler).

HEAD END
The cable company's focal point, from which all programming is integrated and managed, and then sent down via the distribution system to reach the market. Also refers to the transmitter site from which signals are uplinked to a satellite.

IRD
    Integrated Receiver/Descrambler, or a satellite
    (TVRO) receiver with a built-in Videocipher.

LINKABIT
    A supreme engineering center in San Diego, and
    the designer of the original Videocipher sold to
    General Instruments. Now owned by Titan, and
    expected to return to the Videocipher business.

MICROWAVE
    The term used to define the frequency range above
    2 GHz (2,000,000,000 cycles per second). The
    microwave domain is divided into bands, with
    TVRO in either the C-band (about 5-6 GHz or
    Ku-band (about 14 GHz).

MODULE
    A Videocipher module contains all descrambling
    circuitry required for satellite (TVRO) reception.
    Various IRD manufacturers all use the same
    Videocipher module.

OFF-AIR
    Programming radiated by a conventional non-cable
    transmitter and detected with an antenna.

PAY-PER-VIEW

A means by which the subscriber can agree to pay for the privilege of watching specific films or events, and the cable company can then authorize descrambling of that specific program by sending a signal down the cable to all identity codes that correspond to paying viewers. An alternative method uses self-destroying (timed) filters.

REVERSE TRAP

A notch filter that removes deliberate interference that has been added to the signal.

SATELLITE

In the context of television broadcasting, a geostationary (motionless over one point on the earth) satellite about 22,500 miles out, equipped with solar panels for power and transponders to distribute television signals across the pattern created by its antenna.

SEED KEY

A portion of the Videocipher's identity code that, when combined with data transmitted by an authorizing signal, permits descrambling. A SEED KEY EXTRACTOR was a program that could find that information and would therefore support CLONING of the original Videocipher.

STABILIZER (also ENHANCER)
Electrical instrument that removes Copyguard™
or Macrovision™ from pre-recorded videotapes, or
otherwise improves quality from a videotape when
it is being viewed or copied.

SUBCARRIER
In satellite (TVRO), a new signal impressed on the
carrier in addition to video, and usually containing
either data or audio information. Undetectable
by conventional video tuning means.

SYNTHESIZER
A technique by which a desired frequency (TV
channel, for instance) can be tuned with the
accuracy and stability of a crystal, thus eliminating
fine tuning. Advertising uses the terms "PLL,"
"Phase Locked Loop," and "quartz-locked" to refer
to a synthesized tuning method.

TEST CHIP
Vernacular for a chip that, once installed in a
descrambler, either gives it the identity of a
unit authorized to receive all channels (obsolete
in most markets) or generates to the descrambler
circuit the instructions it would ordinarily receive
from a legitimate descrambler when programming
subscriptions have been paid.

THREE MUSKETEERS, or MUSKETEER

A "musketeer" chip is installed in a descrambler for which one legitimate subscription has been purchased. The chip remembers the codes sent to the descrambler circuit to authorize it, and sends the same code for all scrambled programs. The user subscribes to one, and gets all. Thus, "one for all, all for one."

TRANSPONDER

A combined receiver–transmitter on a satellite. It receives a signal from a transmitter on the ground on one frequency, and re-transmits it back to the ground on another frequency. Each transponder represents one video channel, and can also handle a multitude of audio channels simultaneously.

TRAP

A selective filter that removes part of the signal and prevents it from continuing, but passes the rest of the signal unaltered.

TVRO

TeleVision Receive Only. Refers to earth stations, or dish assemblies, for reception of satellite signals only. The vernacular for a TVRO system includes such terms as "satellite system", or "dish".

UPLINK
Signal *from* the earth *to* the transponder.

VIDEO
The "picture" portion of a television signal, as opposed to AUDIO. The VIDEO portion of a scrambled satellite signal is readily descrambled, but the AUDIO is difficult. The AUDIO portion of a cable signal is left unscrambled.

ZAP
The death of a descrambler, resulting from a successful cable or satellite company's counter-measure.

ZERO-ONE-ZERO
The first three digits of an early generation Videocipher that was easy to modify. Later units were numbered 018 and 032, with each stage requiring more effort and better technology to modify than the previous one.

ZERO-ONE-EIGHT
The serial number prefix that identifies last of the easily modified Videociphers.

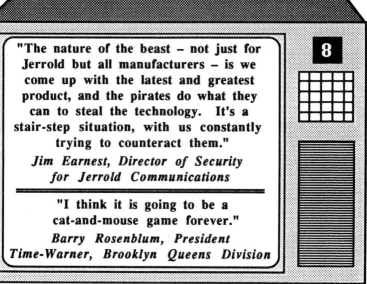

"The nature of the beast – not just for Jerrold but all manufacturers – is we come up with the latest and greatest product, and the pirates do what they can to steal the technology. It's a stair-step situation, with us constantly trying to counteract them."

Jim Earnest, Director of Security for Jerrold Communications

"I think it is going to be a cat-and-mouse game forever."

Barry Rosenblum, President Time-Warner, Brooklyn Queens Division

as reported in *Secure Signals*

APPENDIX A

SPECTRUM ALLOCATION IN NORTH AMERICA

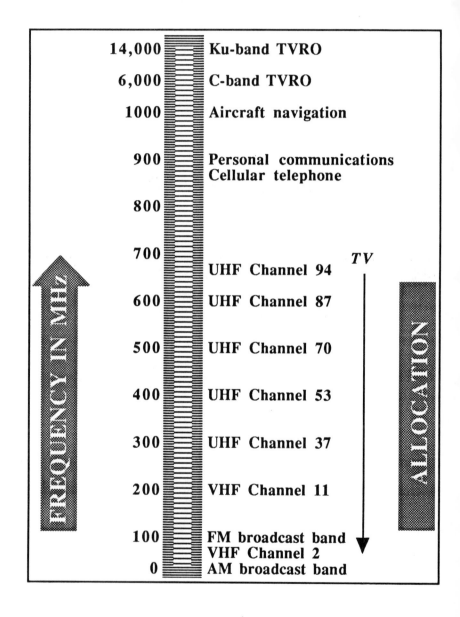

APPROXIMATE FREQUENCIES OF ALL OFF-AIR AND CABLE CHANNELS

Channel   Frequency (MHz)

2 54-60
...add 6 MHz to reach next in series till 6
6 82-88

FM band........... 88-108

A2............... 108-114
A1............... 114-120
A............... 120-126
...add 6 MHz to reach next in series till 13
13............... 210-216

J 216-222
...add 6 MHz to reach next in series till W
W 294-300

AA 300-306
...add 6 MHz to reach next in series till ZZ
ZZ................ 450-456

Channel spacing is 6 MHz

"The gray market is BIG business shaped by the twin pressures of money and the law. In cable alone, annual revenue from sales of hardware and services must exceed $100M."

"Pirate cable has its own rules, and if you don't know them, you get in trouble, yet the only way to learn is by trial and error."

"This is a dangerous business. Threats can come from the feds, the local law, your competitors, the cable companies, and – too often – from your customers."

"When they caught me, the only thing I had to bargain with was my customer list."

Candid comments by distributors of cable descramblers.

APPENDIX B

SUPPLIERS OF SERVICES & PRODUCTS

GRAY MARKET NICHES

• *Is nothing sacred?* Not even Nintendo™ is immune. IRATA (that's either *ATARI* backwards or a truly remarkable coincidence) Systems, at 602-926-7969, offers a video that describes the Nintendo™ cartridge, including the "CIC lock chip", and shows ways to avoid it. They sell parts that support "repairs."

• To fry your neighbor's TV set, try the pocket video jammer offered by Consumertronics, at 505-434-1778.

• Though the FCC strictly limits the power at which all transmitters can operate, many companies offer TV distribution transmitters that *far* exceed the limits set for them by law. Though they interfere with neighbors, they let one cable box or VCR transmit to the whole house. Ads may say "for use only outside the U. S.," but it's no problem placing orders for U.S. destinations.

• To any technologist, advertisements for some television accessories are absolutely legal but utterly embarrassing. Some of the worst are for devices that "turn the entire house into a giant antenna," or others that look like miniature satellite dishes but are actually common rabbit ears (dipoles). The wording in these ads make it appear that the products have repealed the laws of physics. They haven't, but it's obviously profitable to make people think they have...

SUPPLIER DATABASE

The following pages list suppliers of satellite and cable descramblers and associated devices, video "stabilizers," and similar equipment and services that support the television gray market, derived from advertisements. Magazines that print such advertising include:

Car & Driver	313-971-3600
Damark Catalog (Code B393-3152) ...	800-729-9000
Nuts & Volts	800-783-4624
Popular Communications	516-681-2922
Popular Electronics	516-293-3000
Popular Science	212-779-5000
Radio Electronics Magazine	516-293-3000
Video Magazine	800-365-1008

SATELLITE (TVRO) INFORMATION AND EQUIPMENT

Cabletronics 9800 Topanga Canyon Blvd Chatsworth, CA 91311	800-433-2011	Videocipher II Descrambling Manual, software Large selection of gray market manuals, with both information and software for Videocipher
Cathouse	513-528-0707	Bulletin Board on subject satellite systems Up to date information on scrambling, etc.
Electron John	718-987-7617	B-MAC decoders and test chips Expensive - receives signals intended for hotels, racetracks, Vegas betting parlors. Also Australia.
Elite Engineering POB 55 Oswego, NY 13827		Videocipher software, developer kit Free catalog
General Instruments San Diego, CA	800-438-3331	Videocipher manufacturer
La Paz Electronics POB 261095 San Diego, CA 92196	619-586-7610	Videocipher chips, lithium batteries, etc. Suitable for 010, 018, 032 series VCII
No name in advertisement 2316 Channel Dr. Ventura, CA 93003	800-652-0255	TVRO equipment Free Satellite TV Buyers guide
None in advertisement	914-436-5354	B-Mac decoders for adult films, fights, races 011-52-988-33476 to order MultiCinema, The Finish Line. B-Mac descrambler: $1,675.00!!
None in advertisement 1614 Union Valley Rd., Suite W. Milford, NJ 07480	201-728-3217	Videocipher II and II+ repairs, services

SATELLITE (TVRO) INFORMATION AND EQUIPMENT

None in advertisement	900-786-6667	Descrambler codes on monthly basis Monthly audio codes for Videocipher, "intended for testing only." $3.50 per call.
RJ Electronics	616-766-2725	VC-2 old style modules, $325 each tested These modules are easily modified, and plug in to replace newest (and more difficult) modules.
Scrambling News 1552 Hertel Ave. Buffalo, NY 14216	716-874-2088	Satellite newsletter Good insight to gray and legit TVRO equipment markets, legislation, etc.
Summit Box 489 Bronx, NY 10465		Descrambler kits Complete descrambler kit $49.95 + $5 S&H, also sells cable kit.
Telecode POB 6426 Yuma, AZ 85366-6426	602-782-2316	Books, manuals for hackers Catalog $3. Many gray market manuals, books, including cellular, etc.
Testron POB 1000 Huntsville, NY 12406	607-326-7207	Videocipher "test chips", repair services " Test device for Videocipher Plus..." In business many years.
Universal Electronics, Inc. 4555 Groves Rd, Suite 13 Columbus, OH 43232	800-241-8171	Book: Hidden Signals on Satellite TV How to hear/see hidden programming. 240pp, $19.95 + s/h
Walker Technical Services Route 2, Box 662 Catlett, VA 22019	703-788-9123	Services, descrambler repair, batteries In business many years.
Western Technologies POB 2531 Paso Robles, CA 93447		VCII+ schematics, part list, source code Sells video-only test chip *code* for $14.95. Customer must program the chip & install it.

The Television Gray Market

CABLE EQUIPMENT AND INFORMATION

ABC Electronics	800-643-6663	Cable test aids and converters "Bullet proof", quantities 1 - 500
Ace Products	800-234-0726	Free catalog, cable TV boxes - all types
Advantage Electronics 1125 Riverwood Dr Burnsville, MN 55337	800-952-3916	Descramblers: Jerrold, Zenith, Pioneer, etc. All credit cards, "12 years experience"
B&S Sales 46518 Van Dyke #101 Utica, MI 48317	313-790-7896	Descramblers, converters "I don't sell in Michigan. It's company policy".
Boss Distributors POB 1282 Beloit, WI 53511	608-364-1928	Cable boxes Customer must sign statement: "Yes, I'm paying for full service."
C&C Specialties 310-867-0081	800-452-7090	Cable: Test modules for TOCOM "This one works" $69.95. Also advertises as "Cable Test". PM ad: "fully activates unit"
Cable Price Club	800-377-9742	Descramblers "Absolutely the lowest price" & "all major brands". CABLE PRICE CLUB??!!
Cable Ready Company	800-234-1006	Descramblers, etc.

CABLE EQUIPMENT AND INFORMATION

Cable World	800-234-7193	Descramblers GI DPV-7 is $250, SA $150.
Cabletronics 9800 Topanga Canyon Blvd Chatsworth, CA 91311	800-433-2011	Descramblers, hacker literature & manuals Ad says, "CA penal code #593D forbids" shipping to CA customers.
Cabletronics Box 30502 Bethesda, MD 20824		Books, etc. for several gray markets. Manual: how to get "HBO, Showtime, Adult" $12.95
Citywide Enterprises	800-626-1919	Test aids, decoders, high quantities avail "Stop bullet - don't get zapped". Jerrold $299 Video - How to Install Test Aids
CNC Concepts PO Box 34503 Minneapolis, MN 55449	800-535-1843	Descramblers, etc. Ad says "Dealers wanted"
Communications Engineering 76 Boulevard Hudson Falls, NY 12839		Manuals on cable gray market Stamp for catalog
Cyan Electronics	407-952-5064	Zenith test chips $10 in 100 qty
Deca	800-933-2242	Descramblers

CABLE EQUIPMENT AND INFORMATION

E.S. 5765-F Burke Centre Parkway, Burke, VA 22015	Software to **produce** turn-on chips. Info packs and software: $500 for all, no refunds. For Tocom, Zenith, Jerrold, etc.
Electroman POB 24474 New Orleans, LA 70184	Bullet Buster, $19.95 + $3 S/H "Electronic shield" for cable boxes
End Connection 419-243-7856	Illustrated Book of Cable TV, plus test kits "John" – $24.95 cable repair book is better than average. Parts for various descramblers.
Enterprises POB 572 Medford, NY 11763-0572	Descramblers
Freedom Electronics 800-972-2779 3400 NE 12th Ave., Suite 189 Ft Lauderdale, FL 33334	Descramblers Free catalog
General Instruments 800-438-3331 San Diego, CA	Makes Jerrold descramblers Extensive security effort, much more effective than other descrambler mfgrs.
Greenleaf Electronics 708-616-8050 POB 538 Bensenville, IL 60106	Decoders, descramblers Careful disclaimer, yet no Nevada or Illinois sales. Full page ad in Nuts & Volts.
Harrywhite *(one word!)* PO Box 1790 Baytown, TX 77520	Manual: Build Your Own Descrambler - $10 Seven easy steps, $12 in Radio Shack parts, free descrambling methods to try

CABLE EQUIPMENT AND INFORMATION

Intellivideo 1311 El Camino Real, Suite Millbrae, CA 94030	415-583-8283	Descramblers and converters Full page ad, many brands new and used
J.E.S. Inc.	800-676-7966	Descramblers "All equipment 'bullet-proof'"
J&R Electronics	301-927-3461	Chips for Jerrold, SA, Pioneer, Tocom
Jayco Electronics	718-849-8750	Descramblers, test chips
JP Video 1470 Old Country Road, Suite Plainview, NY 11803	800-950-9145	Cable converters and descramblers No New York sales
KD Video POBox 29538 Minneapolis, Minnesota,	800-327-3407	Descramblers Full page ad, including Pioneer, many others
King Wholesale	800-729-0036	Descramblers
L&L Electronics, Inc. 1430 Mier Street, Suite 522 Des Plaines, IL 60016	800-542-8190	Descramblers Credit cards, disclaimer, no Illinois orders

CABLE EQUIPMENT AND INFORMATION

Lake Sylvan Sales	800-800-4582	Descramblers Big advertising budget
Lyn Johnson Electronics	800-779-1761	Descramblers
M. K. Electronics 8362 Pines Blvd. Pembroke Pines, FL 33024	800-582-1114	Descramblers Visa, Mastercard
M&G Electronics, Inc. 301 Westminster St. Providence, RI 02903	800-258-1134	Cable descrambler kits, tutorials, manuals Kits based on Radio Electronics articles: all-mode descrambler, snooperstopper
Marco Electronics PO Box 1475 Las Cruces, NM 88004	800-736-0878	Cable boxes, chips for Zenith, filters ($20) Also sells remotes, "latest circuitry Zeniths"
Midwest Electronics PO Box 5000, Suite 311 Carpentersville, IL 60110	800-648-3030	Decramblers Disclaimer, and no IL orders. 60¢ for catalog
Mike Nelson's Movie View PO Box 26 Wood Dale IL 60191	800-735-5912	Descramblers, etc. Also advertises as "Movie View Sales"
Modular Engineering	615-658-6557	Test aids: Tocom, SA, Jerrold, Starcom, etc. Complete descramblers "Sold as second unit only". Also ads without company name.

CABLE EQUIPMENT AND INFORMATION

Mountain View Sales, Inc.	615-523-7279	Converters, descramblers "Bullet proof"
Mr. Combo	904-625-7726	Test aids, converter/descramblers
Multi-Vision Electronics 2370 S. 123rd Ct, Suite 126 Omaha, NE 68144	800-835-2330	"Bullet proof" "You agree to comply...." Also, "Video Stabilizers Available"
N. E. Engineering	617-770-3830	Test chips
National Cable	219-935-4128	Cable converter/descramblers Also "test modules"
None in advertisement	519-252-1668	Zenith turn on chips, $10 qty 100 "Full service mode including PPV"
None in advertisement 3128 Lake Washington Road, Melbourne, FL 32934		"Test kits" For Zenith, Starcom, Pioneer, Tocom, also tools to open "tamper-proof" boxes.
None in advertisement	305-425-4378	SA, Tocom, Zenith boxes, "all new ZZ chip" "Will beat any price in this magazine"

CABLE EQUIPMENT AND INFORMATION

None in advertisement	800-334-8475	Converters, descramblers, test aids MC/Visa/AMEX
None in advertisement	407-728-4928	Pioneer test aids for 5XXX and 6XXX units 30-day money back guarantee -- $55
None in advertisement	800-742-2273	Chips "Test turn ons", with prices
None in advertisement	615-658-6557	Turn-on test chips. "Will fully activate..." Also ads as "Modular Engineering"
None in advertisement	800-822-9955	Oak M35B: $39.95 Most other types available. COD only.
None in advertisement	800-942-6649	Descramblers: Tocom DPV72, DPVBB72 "All your cable needs"
None in advertisement	800-925-9426	Snooper stopper, $33.95 also wireless video sender, $54.95
None in advertisement	800-872-6585	"Cable devices" - all digital tri-mode pans Contact "Art". Ad says "no tuning, works everywhere"

CABLE EQUIPMENT AND INFORMATION

None in advertisement	518-773-9151	Test chips, bullet proof Most models, plus repair parts and services
None in advertisement California	916-768-3491	Bullet-proofer $19.95 plus shipping
Northeast Electronics PO Box 3310 N. Attleboro, MA 02761	800-886-8699	Snooper Stopper, kits and built. "Protect yourself from descrambler detection and stop the bullet." Credit cards.
Nu-Tek Electronics 3250 Hatch Road Cedar Park TX 78613	800-228-7404	Descramblers, including Pioneer "Dual switching for those difficult areas"
Nu-Vue Electronics 175-B U. S. Highway 1, Suite Tequesta, FL 33469	407-336-8538	Complete descramblers and chips. MCard, Visa, catalog $2
Pacific Cable Co. Inc. 7325 1/2 Reseda Blvd. Reseda, CA 91335	800-345-8927	Descramblers All major credit cards
Panaxis Productions PO Box 130 Paradise, CA 95967	916-534-0417	Product "CTV" is $4, plans for descrambler. Also CTV defeats inband gated sync scrambling. Large (Pancom) catalog with many kits, plans
Pancom International PO Box 130 Paradise, CA 95967		Descramblers (also surveillance electronics) Free catalog

CABLE EQUIPMENT AND INFORMATION

Program International, Inc. PO Box 3734 Ridgewood, NY 11386	800-952-8244	Chips for TOCOM $39.99. "Even unlock new trick modes at fight time"
Redcoat Electronics PO Box 9255 Bolton, CT 06043		Descramblers
Republic Cable Products 4080 Paradise Road, #15 Las Vegas, NV 89109	800-648-7938	Descramblers Special prices for dealers
SAC	800-622-3799	Descramblers Zenith boxes, already modified, $189
Scorpion	407-722-5749	Zenith test chips, models ST1000 thru 5000 $39.95. Also other test chips, claims "wholesale prices."
Skyline Systems 114 S. Euclid Ave. Park Ridge, IL 60068	800-243-3967	Descramblers Credit cards, all models
Star Circuits PO Box 94917 Las Vegas, NV 89193	800-535-7827	Tunable notch filters, $16 Suitable for traps, reverse traps. Also for interference.
Summit Box 489 Bronx, NY 10465		Descrambler kits Complete descrambler kit $44.95 + $5 S&H, also sells satellite kit

Appendix B

CABLE EQUIPMENT AND INFORMATION

Sun Coast	904-625-9545	Cable descramblers "Absolutely no Florida sales"
Surplus City Box 25301 Little Rock, AR 72221		Service: will duplicate any memory chips Advertised in CABLE section of Nuts & Volts
Surplus Electronics PO Box 10009 Colorado Springs, CO 80932		Manuals Tocom schematics, secrets, software
Tamper-Bit Supply Co.	310-866-7125	Tools to remove tamper-proof screws TOCOM 5503 and 5507 bits
Ted Hex	800-TEDHEX	Chips for descramblers Knowledgeable
Telecable	216-497-8901	Descramblers 24 hours, "dealers only", no Ohio slaes
Telecode POB 6426 Yuma, AZ 85366-6426	602-782-2316	Cable test chip software Publishes books and "hacker" manuals, also
Telecode POB 6426 Yuma, AZ 85366-6426	602-782-2316	Manual for cable hackers Catalog $3. Also: Black Box Bible $34.95. Many gray market manuals, books.

CABLE EQUIPMENT AND INFORMATION

TKA Electronics	800-729-1776	Descramblers Free catalog: Oak, Zenith, Tocom, SA, Jerrold
U. S. Cable 4100 N. Powerline Rd Pompano Beach, FL 33073	800-772-6244	Descramblers "Bullet proof", but requires a disclaimer and no FL sales
Universal Products	404-740-0711	Descramblers: Scientific Atlanta Model 8580 "Wholesale" at $235, with remote
Vega One Electronics PO Box 71465 Las Vegas, NV 89170-1465	702-253-1852	Cable converter/descramblers Buyer must sign long disclaimer/waiver, but still no Nevada sales. Full page ad.
Video Proof PO Box 60035 King of Prussia, PA 19406	800-597-0886	Descramblers, test chips "of course", bulletbuster Half-page ad, Channel mapping info, also
West Coast Electronics	800-628-9656	Descramblers Hamlin at $44 each, qty 10
Worldwide Cable 1291 Powerline Road, Suite Pompano Beach, FL 33069	800-772-3233	Descramblers, converters Free catalog, but "No Florida Sales"
Z-Mann Cable Supply Florida	407-862-5878	Everything, incl filters, repair parts, chips "If you live within Florida, don't waste your dime and my time." Chips $11.25 ea, qty 100!

VIDEOTAPE COPY PROTECTION REMOVAL

Damark PO Box 29900 Minneapolis, MN 55429-0900	800-729-9000	Digital Video Stabilizer "...may be against certain federal and state copyright laws"
Fordham	800-695-4848	Stabilizer "Copyguard stabilizer, removes all Copyguard from video..." $39.95 + $6.95 S&H
Jayco Ventures, Inc. 4072 NE 8th Ave Fort Lauderdale, FL 33334	305-563-6585	Video copy protection remover
Many stores in your neighborhood carry these products.....		Video Copyguard removers A walk through a typical mall will probably locate several sources for such equipment.
Nu-Tek Electronics 3250 Hatch Road Cedar Park TX 78613	800-228-7404	Video stabilizer Also sells cable descramblers, etc.
Radio Shack all		Videotape enhancer/stabilizer
Roger's Specialist 27712 Pinehills Ave. Santa Clarita, CA 91351	800-366-0579	#VA-154 Copyguard Corrector at $49
Zentek 3670-12 West Oceanside Road Oceanside, NY 11572	800-445-9285	Stabilizer, Copyguard remover

Some consumers have convinced themselves that programming theft cannot be a very serious business, since "they put it on the cable no matter what I do, and I'd never actually subscribe to all those services, so no one really loses anything."
They are wrong...

In California, the consumer can be sentenced to a $1,000 fine or 90 days jail term for the first offense, and is also liable to the cable operator for three times damages plus attorney fees.

A seller of descramblers and/or chips to modify them
– *within California* –
can receive a $10,000 fine for the first offense, and then a $20,000 fine *plus* up to one year in jail for the second offense.

California Penal Code 593d
...and there are similar penalties in most states.

INDEX